The Good Ol' Boys

Lorraine Kieffer

19
9
6

The
Good Ol' Boys

by William H. Hull

Illustrations by Victoria Hayen

The story of Billy Boy, a lad growing up in a small mid-America town in the twenties and thirties, of his experiences with others and his development into manhood. Herein are shown the influences which shaped his life and personality.

Written in a conversational, easy-to-read style.

Table of Contents

Preface

This is not my first book. It's my seventh. No, the eighth because we won't count the one I withdrew from publishing several years ago. In many ways I find myself excited about this new one.

Just as a mother contemplates the delivery of her child, viewing it with great concern, with love, hoping she can nurture it into a successful adult, so do I as writer, worry over the possibilities, hoping this work will be meaningful to the readers. Not because of any possible financial profit but, like that mother, just wanting to produce something of value.

But this book is more than that. It's an historical recording of a period of relative quiet in our country, the days following the first world war when great sociological changes were occurring. That period just before and yet during the Great Depression, those simple years when the country was trying to reabsorb its returning veterans of the war that was to end all wars and to open the west for final expansion. A time before the caravan of poor people, wrongly universally called "Okies," headed for California.

It was a time of adult partying, of childhood confusion during the movement from agrarian to urban life in midwestern USA, a time of introducing life—changing devices like the radio and the washing machine, the great change between butchering and curing your own meat to having great packing houses do it and making it readily available, fresh at any time. A time when children still sat around in the yard near the house and played, oblivious to the factors which would change their lives so completely.

It was a time when the automobile and the truck replaced horse-drawn vehicles, a time when huge traveling circuses rolled into town on trains, to set up their big tops and to parade down Main street with lumbering elephants and screaming calliopes.

Yet it was also an era of great contrast in family life. In the Louisiana bayous a child captured birds by laying a slipknot noose in an open yard, liberally baited with cracked corn. When a bird stepped into the noose the hidden girl would give a quick pull on the string to snare the bird. It didn't matter what kind the bird, she told me many years later. Whatever, sparrow, dove, bluebird, blackbird, crow, one and all they went into the family cooking pot as a source of meat.

Meanwhile, far away in Canada a young girl's father commissioned a blacksmith to make him a roasting pan so big it almost filled the family cooking oven. It needed to be big to handle the huge roasts and the occasional suckling pig which was slow roasted to perfection. That family lived well. The daughter lived to exceed a hundred years.

I had awakened at three-thirty one morning to question where I was heading with this book. I knew there was a lot to say but why select Billy Boy to talk about? Why not Charlie, or Mamie, or Maribelle? Because I knew Billy Boy's stories and prayed I could make them interesting to others, either because of nostalgia or because of a reader's interest in a way of life which was long gone before he was born.

My decision: there's a lot to tell. Go on with it, man, but delve into the little things that truly constitute life. Things like trying to catch a bird with a string, just for food, trying to do something mischievous on Halloween while still staying within permissive limits, trying to bake a mud-covered potato in a can in an open fire, trying to save all of those first real tastes of life.

Why the title—*The Good Ol' Boys*—you may ask? Because as I lived in the mid-south and traveled much in the deep south, whenever I heard the term "good ol' boy" it was with warmth and kindness, which is the way I feel about the growing up and aging of Billy Boy. True, there is another side of this expression wherein the user puts down the good ol' boy as being overbearing, crude, loud, and/or gullible. In no way is that sort of inference meant here; I'm speaking only of the kind of person I'd like to have as a friend.

Childhood Years

Billy Boy

Aunt Gladys, Dad's sister, was one of my favorite aunts. She came to the house one day, met me at the door and gaily exclaimed, "How are you, Billy Boy?" At that moment all of my pent-up anger (kids always seem to have pent up anger stored just beneath the surface) came boiling up and I said somewhat rudely, "Don't call me Billy Boy. My name is Bill." After that I was Bill. Billy was a sissified little kid's nickname and I was too grown up to carry that stigma.

Aunt Gladys probably had her burdens to carry also. She had married and brought an outsider into the family of six siblings—four boys and two girls, counting herself. It wasn't that the outsider was not a likable man, or that he couldn't really get accepted into the clan of four brothers. It was that he was, of all things, a Democrat!

That's a capital D—Democrat. And this family was Republican. Grandfather Charlie (their father) had served the county as assessor for eight years, just before I was born, and as sheriff for four years after my birth. And he must have been Republican through and through. So Gladys' husband, John, had to put up with the kidding and putting down by his Republican brothers-in-law. This was particularly touchy during the Franklin Delano Roosevelt presidential years when John thought Roosevelt was God and some of his brothers in law thought Roosevelt was that X!+&%#!* man in the White House.

We moved from the house on McRoberts street when I was about eight years old. Although it had been the only home I had known I felt no sorrow in leaving it. Many things had happened there. Those little boy experiences of growing up still are in my memory over sixty years later. Along with the good memories of playing with neighborhood kid friends, there were some bad memories. I had been punished for throwing a snowball with a rock center through the Humpfeldt's window; I had been shot in the face with a twenty-two pistol. And my beloved brother, Charles, had died while we lived there.

I remember the details of that house on McRoberts Street so well that I tried to get my father to go back to the house with me, after sixty years so I could give him a detailed layout of each room; where the furniture sat, where the "library table" was placed, exactly where the big heater with the isinglass windows was placed, the table on which my dad tinkered with the crystal radio which brought people from all over town to hear for the first time talk and music "all the way from Kansas City—108 miles away." Those were fascinating days.

In one way I had declared my first independence there too, at about eight years of age.

And the family no longer called me "Billy Boy."

Our Home

It was a small house, that one on McRoberts street, where I spent my first eight years, but it was a comfortable house, largely due to my mother's personality. The singing, the love expressed, the freshly baked foods all created an aura that a child won't forget.

There were only four rooms and a bath but we did quite well with them. They were parlor, bedroom, kitchen/dining and the extra room which would be called a family room today.

Furniture was of the era or even older, mainly being very heavy and predominately made of oak.

The parlor, which one entered directly from the front door had the usual chairs, plus a large leather covered couch, a library table and a Victrola. Why that table was called a "library table" I never knew because it had nothing to do with books nor library in our house. Probably about two by four feet in top size, it had heavy legs which turned out into a pattern any antiquer could describe correctly. But that table was heavy, so heavy, so solidly built I've often thought it could have been taken outside and used as a chopping block. It could have withstood the tremendous blows of an axe coming down on a burl.

In one corner was the Victrola; probably almost every house had one. It was spring fed by winding it up, had a large flat spinning table with a needle that very seldom was changed, no matter how badly it scratched. But everyone had a few songs of the day, like "My Blue Heaven" and numbers by the greats like Caruso. Of course there was a carpet on the floor. Not wall-to-wall carpeting, you understand, but a center carpet with an edge of hardwood floor around the carpeting.

The living room had a big heating stove in the middle of the room, with a natural clustering of chairs around it. Against a wall was my father's tinkering table where he worked on his crystal radio. People from all over town would come by to hear Aubrey Hull's radio pick up Kansas City, 108 miles away. It was a thrill for all of us. People liked my dad. He was of the people, one of the real Good Ol' Boys.

Kitchens were utilitarian, dominated by a fairly large table and a large cookstove much like my grandmother's, described elsewhere in this book. This one burned coal, which had to be brought up from the basement in a coal-bucket. That rascal could put out so much heat it was uncomfortable to eat at the nearby table. Of course there was an old fashioned cupboard or china closet to hold the dishes, as well as a flour cabinet with spices too. One half of the top contained a bin for flour, which was sifted through a built-in funnel into a bowl or cup at the bottom and then closed off by a rolltop front, much like that on a rolltop desk. It had a work level front shelf and pan storage at the bottom.

The bedroom contained two full size double beds, one for my parents and one for Charles and me. They were the traditional iron framework beds, which dad painted occasionally, a mattress and coil springs resting on slats, very similar to today's beds.

Of course a chair or two, one a rocking chair which I still possess, and a dresser. Dressers were simply three- or four-door chests with a large mirror suspended on the top in such a manner it could be tilted to provide best makeup angles.

The bathroom was just another bathroom, containing

the usual claw-footed bathtub and "inside plumbing" which really meant an inside toilet. Thank goodness it was new enough to have a flushing handle like today's toilets rather than one of those chain-pull devices; for those the water tank was very high, near the ceiling, and featured a handle on a long chain which, when pulled, permitted water to drop down through the pipe to flush the toilet. It was as modern as it could be.

VICTORIA

The Coal Bucket Incident

I, Billy Boy, was a climber.

My foot was balanced on the top rung of a chair back tipped against the wall, near the kitchen range, and my other foot was atop the cold range, as I stretched my little eight-year old frame to reach the cookies in the cabinet just out of reach.

The chair moved. Both feet moved. I crashed down onto the coal bucket and blood spurted everywhere.

Probably coal buckets are found today only in remote areas but years ago they were necessary utensils.

Coal came from a corner of the cellar or a basement, via a chute from the coal truck., via a train from Illinois.

It was hauled to the stoves in a bucket, a miserable metal bucket built so the contents could be dumped from the front chute into the firebox of a stove or sometimes shoveled out with a small shovel, or even hand-picked pieces removed with the fingers.

It had a handle suspended across the top, joined on the bucket with hinged-like pieces of metal about the size of a half dollar. When the handle was limp, these hinges projected straight up like round knives. And they were so thin they were sharp.

They were not meant for a small boy to fall on from some feet up in the air.

Like I did.

That darned coal bucket jumped up and got me in the face. Or perhaps I landed on the bucket when I fell, slashing open my chin. Believe it, the blood did flow.

To this day I carry a scar on my chin, souvenir of the coal bucket incident.

Hammering on the Door

Bang! Bang! So went his hammer on the front door. eight times he hammered tacks into our front door. Then he stood back, admired his work, and started to leave the porch.

He was a huge man, not only big in frame but fat, not unusual for the middle-aged son of a German family. As he crossed the wooden porch it creaked ominously as if it too were saying "Ouch."

There on the door he left two signs, each a foot square. The green one contained one large word: QUARANTINED, followed by words like "Keep out as long as posted," etc. After all, this was a pest house at that moment.

The other sign simply said SCARLET FEVER. But sometimes it said MEASLES or SMALL POX, or DIPHTHERIA, or maybe MUMPS. Whatever infectious disease was present, it was announced to the world.

Every medical doctor must have had a roomful of these signs and they covered nearly every possible ailment except RUNNING NOSE or ALLERGY. Obviously, they were for the infectious, highly contagious diseases.

Even in those days the expression "Whatever goes around, comes around" was meaningful because every childhood infectious disease came around, being spread through classrooms, Sunday schools, movie houses, birthday parties, wherever kids came together.

And I think we had them all.

Of course those quarantine signs stayed posted until the doctor authorized their removal. In the meantime the family of children and non-breadwinners stayed closed up in the house. The breadwinner was permitted to go to and fro to his job, but he was the only one. I don't remember whether home deliveries of milk, bread and ice were permitted but controls were quite strict.*

Today, when the world is on the doorstep of the twenty-first century, it's hard to believe how few tools a physician had in his armamentarium sixty years ago.

Just observe how the use of these quarantine signs disappeared very soon after the discovery and use of penicillin.

After all, it had barely been sixty years since Clara Barton, "the Angel of the Battlefield" during the civil war had earned the love of thousands who benefited from her nursing care on the battlefronts. Nursing as a profession hadn't even been around for many years.

Only about a lifetime previously, in 1836, a young lady named Florence Nightingale wanted to enter an Infirmary (school) to enroll in a three months course in "Health" (notice the word "nursing" was not used.) When Florence suggested this to her family it created quite a scene. Her mother rebelled at such a proposal and her sister actually became hysterical.

So health care was indeed in its infancy.

Today's well cared for populations in the progressive nations apparently have no idea how their great grandmothers sat on stools to deliver their babies, how their grandfathers went through horrible battlefield amputations, many times without any anesthesia.

The simple maladies and procedures of today, such as appendicitis, were frequently death blows in those days. It has been said the surgery on my brother, Charles Hull (1916–1926), would have been successful and his life spared, for twenty-five cents worth of penicillin, not available then. Without it, he died.

Medical museums today have collections of those old doorpost quarantine signs which were common sights in the first third of this century.

---

* Discussed on August 24, 1992 by telephone with Leonard Wilson, MD, University of Minnesota Medical School (624-4416) and with S. Lane Arey, MD, retired physician who practiced in Excelsior, MN from 1923 to 1952 and who was also Excelsior MN Health Officer (926-7100).

The Chicken Ring

What I wanted most when I was five was a chicken ring. Of course that was a long time ago and modern kids don't have chicken rings any more. I pity them.

I had one once. It was blue and coiled around my finger in a glory that was hard to describe. Man, was I proud of that ring. It kept falling off because my finger was too small, so I tried to put it onto my thumb, spreading the ring slightly to make it fit, but then it broke. And when a chicken ring breaks there's nothing to do but throw it away.

To make it worse, Carl, who was older than me, had a yellow chicken ring which he managed to keep for weeks on end without breaking and once Archie Howell had a red one, which was probably the finest thing in the world to own, next to a chicken pulleybone.

And how badly I wanted that chicken ring.

I badgered my mother constantly. As she flew around the kitchen in the morning fixing breakfast I would say "Can I have a chicken ring today?" but she'd only shush me, not realizing that this was a major need in my life equivalent to a new dress for her.

At family gatherings I thought I had a better chance. We were all at my grandfather's house for somebody's birthday and I thought surely with all of those farmers there, someone would have a chicken ring. I even looked at those big tanned fingers, but they were too large to hold such a ring. At least they would know what I meant.

Aunt Gladys came up to me and said, "What do you want, Billy?" In ecstasy never met before in my life, I knew someone finally would grant me The Wish. The Fairy God-mother was here! I said "I want a chicken ring." She immediately turned toward the big kitchen while I jumped with joy. In her stride was purpose and decision. "Here you are, Billy, now say thank you," and she handed me a chicken *wing*. I threw it on the floor, although it was still warm from the frying pan, cried and yelled. After that I got a spanking and was put to bed on grandfather's quilt, covering that deep feath-erbed which was so hot and smothering. I didn't get any chicken at all.

They didn't come in cereal boxes, as they might for to-day's kids. In fact we didn't have cereal boxes with prizes and things to fascinate us. All we had was oatmeal and Cream of Wheat, both of which I truly detested. After all, you eat oat-meal once and it's the same for the rest of your life.

Archie Howell knew everything. Archie was about five years older than I. He could outrun anyone on the block; he even went to school. He was a big boy and was nice to me, the shrimp on the block. I took my problem to Archie and said, "I sure want a chicken ring." Archie, on his way to school, simply said, "Sure, kid, I'll get you one today." Then he walked away.

All day long I was miserable. I couldn't eat my noon sandwich because I was so upset. My mother thought I was sick and was about to douse me with something until I con-vinced her I was okay. I played in the dirt at the corner of the house; I bragged to Julius Humpfeldt that Archie was going to get me a chicken ring. I was scared stiff that Archie didn't really mean it or that he would simply forget.

Finally he got home and I ran over there as fast as my five-year-old legs would go. "Give it to me. Give it to me.

Give it to me," I yelled. Archie reached in his pocket and pulled out a fist which I pried open and THERE IT WAS! A RED CHICKEN RING.

He had stopped at the hatchery and obtained one from someone, probably telling them it was for a little pest in his block.

Of course you know what a chicken ring is. It's a band of colored material (some precursor of plastic) in ring shape. The two ends are tapered and spring apart to go over a chicken's leg for quick identification. I suppose farmers put them on the leg of a hen to mark it for Sunday dinner, to take it to market, for any of several reasons. But to us kids they were chicken rings, those glorious, colorful prizes. A farmer probably bought a zillion of them for fifty cents but we town kids couldn't find one . . . well . . . rarely.

So I finally had my chicken ring.

That night at dinner I held my hand out for dad to see my new ring with the red glowing on my pale hand. "Look, daddy, my new chicken ring." He made me take it off because it was probably dirty. But that night I slept with it tightly clasped in my hand.

Too tightly. During the night I broke it.

Mud Up to the Axle

"You never know what it's like to lose a child," said Barbara, an eighty-five-year-old friend. She was reminiscing about losing a twenty-two-year-old son many years in the past. "It's terrible," she continued. "I just about went crazy, probably should have been hospitalized. Of course I was much younger then, but for a couple of years I was simply crazy with grief."

That helps me understand better the pain that my mother encountered in January, 1926 when her firstborn, my brother Charles, died after emergency surgery for a burst appendix. In today's world it has been said that a quarter's worth of penicillin would have saved his life, had it only been available in those years.

Of course, I was a little kid, two years younger than my big brother, a kid who understood nothing of death and funerals.

But my memories are stark and rather horrible. There had to be a funeral in the First Baptist church of Madison; that would have been a must. Then there was the interment at the Pilot Grove cemetery, in the town of that name, probably twenty miles away.

I can remember well the cemetery trip, the trip in those early vehicles. That route took us out to what later became U.S. Highway 40, a major cross-country road. In those days it wasn't even paved and in Missouri that meant mud.

The funeral cortege traveled that road until it reached the cutoff road to Pilot Grove, also dirt, but in all reality it was mud. I can still hear and visualize the hearse struggling in the mud as it preceded us. Mother, Dad and I sat in the special family car and my Mother cried almost all the way. After all, it was her darling little Charles who was dead.

The mud became worse, having been churned by cars and farm wagons for days. The hearse skidded. Our car skidded. Repeatedly we thought we were all going into the deeply graded ditches along the road, but we didn't.

We only stopped when the hearse stopped, mired to the axles in that heavy gumbo. People got out of their cars to help push the hearse. My Dad was among them.

I recall my mother telling him not to get out, but he would have none of that, so he got out, best clothes, best dress shoes, and all. Probably his only suit.

They all found a spot from which to push and everyone quite kindly let my father get behind a rear wheel. My Dad was not stupid but undoubtedly, not thinking too well, overlooked the danger in which he placed himself. The wheels spun, the mud covered my Dad from head to foot, including the best clothes. What a mess he was when he came back to the car.

From there on, nothing made much impact on this eight-year-old kid. Nothing could top that mess. I don't remember seeing my brother in a casket, nor witnessing it being lowered into the grave; all became subservient in my mind to my Dad's mud-covered appearance.

Perhaps it is just as well.

The Flower Box

It was a unique box. I've never seen anything like it else-where anywhere in my world from Panama, to New Orleans' Lafayette cemetery, to Mexico, to California, or to New England.

It was about twelve by fourteen inches by six inches deep with a removable glass front. Beneath that glass were placed handmade paper flowers to decorate my brother's gravesite.

Artificial flowers weren't available in 1926 but my parents wanted off-season flowers on little Charles' grave to show their love and their loss.

So dad built the box from one-inch pine, painted it, and mother made the paper flowers with great skill. They changed the flowers as the sun bleached them white or as they were stolen. It was thought that the poor people living in nearby ramshackle houses stole flowers from the cemetery, but I could never believe that accusation because they all seemed so nice.

My brother, older by two years, had died at age ten, in 1926, and joined a huge number of predecessors in the Pilot Grove cemetery. My folks purchased a lot for the four of us, at Charles' death, under a small adjoining soft maple tree. It was my role to see both parents interred there, mother in 1966, and dad in 1986, when the maple had grown so large the roots needed severe pruning to provide burial space. The fourth space, intended for me, will probably never be used.

Recently I sat there on a tombstone of a person unknown to me and reminisced how dad and I would pick up the wind-pruned debris from the maple tree, how we tried planting different ground covers to be naturalized in the intense shade of the maple, and the hot summer sun, how we remembered mama and Charles and how tears came to our eyes as we thought of past days.

Although there are more people buried in the Pilot Grove cemetery than there are alive today in the town, it's probably not unique in that respect.

It is unique in the number of Hulls and Moores (mother's family) resting there.

When I walk through that beautiful cemetery today and am overcome by the fall reds and yellows of the trees I can't help thinking of my father making that box for artificial flowers and my mother lovingly curling those paper rose petals to tell the world about her lost firstborn son.

It may be easier and quicker today to buy those plastic flowers and to stick them in a vase at the cemetery but it just isn't the same.

Although the deceased may not know the difference, I'm convinced those left behind feel somewhat cheated by "progress."

We are only what our ancestors passed on to us.

VICTORIA

The Cemetery at Pilot Grove

The town of Pilot Grove, Missouri, was named because during Conestoga wagon days the large number of huge trees at that location was a beacon, a landmark to wagon trains, a pilot's mark to guide them on their way. Added to its pleasant camping facilities were ample water and comparative safety from roaming Indians, so it became known as Pilot Grove.

Just about everybody in my family, on both paternal and maternal sides, who ever lived and died in the county, is buried in that cemetery. There must be between forty and four hundred of them, and most of them were Good Ol' Boys.

My paternal family back to Richard Romulus Hull can be found there. Born in 1829 in Virginia, Richard brought his whole family, including Winston-Salem N.C. wife Louisa Jane Swain, across the country in 1865, by covered wagon. They stopped in Indiana in 1868 for my grandfather, Charles Grant Hull, to be born. I knew him as a man who liked his southern bourbon and his tobaccy, a big, rough, loving grandfather.

Like the Biblical people, the Hulls begat and begat, with Richard begatting five boys and four girls. Later, Charles and wife Sarah Lillian Ashmead had four boys and three girls. Almost all of these people multiplied and started burying their dead in the Pilot Grove cemetery.

The next generation, my parents, Aubrey Grant Hull and

Mary Ann Moore, and their many siblings repeated the process and the cemetery became a family resting place, as it was for many other families.

I can see granddad's gravesite over there, along with that of his sister, my great Aunt Zettie, the woman who created a locally famous salve which cured any sore on man or beast. Also there is Grandfather's brother, Will, a railroad engineer famous in our minds.

On my mother's side are the Moores and the Donahoes, headed by grandparents Frank Moore and Catherine Donahoe Moore. Frank, who died in my father's arms, suffered from dropsy (today called congestive heart failure) and Catherine, my grandmother, who was left to raise eleven children by herself.

Over there is Aunt Fannie, one of Catherine's older offspring, who helped support the family as a schoolteacher. How my daughters giggled over having an aunt named "Fannie." She injured her leg on a sharp corner of a school desk and later died of cancer. Note that people called it her "limb" because it wasn't appropriate to speak of a lady's "leg."

Beyond that stone my dad can see the grave of his baby sister, Madaline, who died on her third birthday. Among other, I find my own mother and brother.

I don't want to be maudlin about that cemetery but have an obligation to say a little more about it, how it became a family resting place. That big old maple tree on our family plot is a symbol of the entire facility, so large its roots had invaded the burial plot that my father's grave preparation in 1986 was a root-pruning affair.

As I said, I could remember the many times Dad and I had pruned the lower branches of that tree to make it possible to move around under it when decorating my mother's and brother's gravesites. Like a large number of small-town or rural cemeteries, the association seems to do nothing in the way of tree trimming, mainly just mowing and general cleaning up.

But I won't continue. I only wish you, dear reader, could sit with me in the solitude of that quiet place and we could talk about Baby Dolly, about Uncle Joe, about all the wonderful Moores who seemed to die en masse during my teens almost as if from an epidemic.

What is the meaning of strolling through a cemetery when everywhere you turn you see a family name? In my case—Hull, Moore, Steger, Davis, Cornelius, Donahoe. Does it assure me of good roots? Does it make me appreciate those who went before? Those who made life easier for us today? It should.

Does it teach me humility? It should. Does it deepen my secure belief in the future? It should. And it should help me retain good memories of beloved people I knew in the past. It does.

The Tree the Giant Peed On

Pilot Grove, Missouri, is a beautiful little town, like everything else in my boyhood. In the twenties it had become about the same population as it remains today.

My Grandmother Moore lived there when I was a child, in a little white house on a side street, complete with a huge garden, a grape arbor, a new storm cellar and a tree that a giant had peed on.

Or at least that was what we were told. Was it my Uncle Bob (Mother's brother) or one of my older cousins who told us the story? There it stood in front of the little home, its magnificence reaching to the sky, its roots tilting the slab of the concrete walk that separated it from the house. I don't know whether it was a catalpa, an elm, or a soft maple, but I suspect the latter. A beautiful tree with lots of foliage, but marred badly by the huge scalded area that ran down the trunk to the ground. The ugly scar was caused by the giant who had peed on the tree. We didn't know nicer terms like "urinated on." It had been peed on. And it was a repulsive sight.

Why wouldn't we believe the story? We believed in giants just as we did in Santa Claus, God, Peter Rabbit, the good fairy, the devil, and ghosts. A five year old in those guileless days would accept anything an elder told him. So we knew it was true. Besides, we could see it ourselves and seeing has always been believing in Missouri.

The scar was there. The raw wood was visible where the bark and the cambian layers had been destroyed by the giant's pee. It was an awesome sight. We kids gathered under it and stared at the wound, realizing no farm animal could have done this. It was true. It had to be a giant.

Occasionally in the spring when we gathered at Grandmother's for a funeral—there were always funerals at Grandmother's—someone would call us to say, "He's been there again," and we'd rush to the tree to see the evidence. Sure enough, there it was. The tree was freshly wet and soiled. It was an event rivaling the funeral.

We never did know the truth. As we grew older, we started hearing adult stories. The tree had been hit by lightning and had been badly scarred. Or was it simply that, typical of older maples, a crotch far up in the tree had permitted sap to run down the bark and ruin it? It was like hearing there really isn't a Santa Claus. Logic finally makes one accept it, but one turns one's back because it is better to believe. So we gradually quit being fascinated, but even as we grew older, even when we reached our teens, we never saw that tree without remembering it as the tree the giants peed on.

Today it is gone. Age, lightning and urine finally forced its removal.

Oranges and Hard Candy

As a child that's what Christmas meant—oranges and hard candies. But, wait, let me say something else first.

The First Baptist church of Madison is still there; I could go into it blindfolded and lead one to every square inch of that fine old brick building, particularly if I entered through the side entrance and providing there hasn't been some major remodeling.

As I mention elsewhere in this book, that is where my teens were spent under the leadership of teacher Jim Farris, God rest his soul. But the younger years were there too. Now we're talking about little boy years, those years when we sat in Sunday School classes coloring pictures or listening to the same stories of Jesus feeding multitudes, bringing the dead back to life and, most of all, of Jesus' great gift to us on the cross.

Of course Christmas was the main event of the year, the focal period, when we presented pageants, dressed as shepherds, wise men, or angels. When we sang in unison before our preening parents, with such songs as "Jesus Loves Me," "Brighten Your Corner" and other oldies.

Santa Claus came to church on Sunday, as well as to the Main street on a Saturday. Today I think it's gradually changed to Friday because it's a better business day. But to us it was more important that Santa Claus came to church.

Why? Because of the goodies he brought for us. Those

goodies were always the same. In retrospect I think the church must have purchased hard candies in hundred pound lots, using them over a several year period, storing them in a hot attic each year until the next Christmas. They were so sticky they formed a mass in our sacks or in our pockets; they were so sweet we loved them but we all probably had what today is called a sugar high from them.

But, also, there were oranges. An orange as a Christmas gift wouldn't mean much to a modern child, but it did to us, because oranges weren't on the market in Madison. One couldn't just go down to Ruskin's store and buy oranges. They didn't exist. Ruskin's had barrels of salt, of pickles, of peanut butter, large cans of many items, boxes of cookies with hinged glass lids so you could buy therefrom. (These are still available in certain spots of the country.) But no oranges. Probably it was a transportation problem to get them to the midwest. Hence they were a great treat for us, even more than the candy. To this day I find a fresh, juicy cold orange one of life's true treats.

And, of course, that church, being Southern Baptist, believed the only acceptable type of baptism was by immersion. None of this sprinkling stuff for us. I may have had a ceremonial baptism as an infant, but doubt it. To us baptism occurred when you accepted Christ and were dunked by the minister.

I well remember when some of us as young teenagers went through that experience. A committee, probably of deacons, kept us in line in a hall outside the baptistry until we were led in one at a time. I was taller than the reverend who was to baptize me. He must have been a strong man to take us one at a time, say the correct words over us, and then lay us down into the water and bring us up quickly, dripping and sputtering like mad. It wasn't an experience we wanted to repeat.

We were lucky because in those days many groups were

immersing in rivers and creeks, while we had a lovely indoor baptistry in a heated building, usually so overheated that it was stifling and everyone sweat.

But that orange, oh what a treat.

Chased by a Blue Racer Snake

Our extended Hull family had glorious get-togethers. Usually it was on someone's birthday, a national holiday, maybe even just a dull Sunday—and we all gathered at my Grandparent Hull's place for fun and dinner.

Maybe it was just to pick those delicious pecans, the hard-shelled variety that grew in granddad's front acreage. Maybe it was just a nowhere-else day and someone got on the phone and we all assembled. Those family events where everyone brought something to eat, a hot dish, ice for making homemade ice cream, or something else tasty.

Occasionally we went somewhere quite different, like on a picnic. On one occasion we went to a little creek valley known as Blue Springs, not the city of Blue Springs in Jackson county near Kansas City, but something more local in Fulton county, a gorgeous place with deep blue water.

It was one of the most beautiful little valleys I have ever seen, featuring a courteous little creek with fish meandering nearby up against the usual Missouri rock wall. Along that wall for about thirty feet someone had carved out a walk—rock on one side, water on the other. it reached a spring which gently bubbled from the wall into the creek.

We kids loved it. There was something different to do. Run. Just run. There were a whole bunch of us, memory says, so it must have included some cousins like Elaine.

VICTORIA

Anyway, we ran, played tag, and raced through the weeds in this flat little valley.

At one time I went screaming back to where the adults sat on blankets on the grass, because a snake was chasing me. It had reared its ugly head and actually chased me as fast as it could slither and I could run, which was wide-open.

As I went screaming for the adults, my Uncle Roy (a brother to Dad) jumped up and interceded, chasing the snake away.

Of course there were comments that I was overly excited, to be kindly, but Uncle Roy spoke up.

"Nope, Billy was right. It was a blue racer and blue racers do chase people. Bill, they particularly like little boys and girls because they can grab them by the heels and swallow them completely. You were lucky, my boy."

That was Roy, the kidder of the family, the very talented craftsman who could make cabinets equal to the best professionally made ones today. Had he lived in a city he would have been a skilled, union cabinet maker, because he had the skill to get it done. If ever there were an example of the Good Ol' Boy it was Roy Hull, that casual, easy going fellow whom everybody loved.

Snakes were not scarce in Missouri. Most of us, children and adults alike, had seen enough cottonmouths, water moccasins, black snakes, and an occasional rattler, to have great respect for them, maybe even fear.

VICTORIA

Doesn't She Look Natural?

Death is a natural event. Adults know that it comes to all of us, that sometimes it is the reward and the release. It can often be traumatic and unpleasant.

All of the deaths that occurred in my family when I was a wee child, except my own brother's, were of my mother's siblings. They were unpleasant because the services were repulsive to me.

Today when I think of Pilot Grove, Missouri, I think of the funerals that occurred so frequently there, and the cemetery full of my many relatives. There were many of them because my mother's brothers and sisters seemed to die at young ages and in a short span of time. Although they were of the same generation as those in my father's family, they had misfortunes that caused early deaths.

Deaths and funerals sixty years ago in that area were probably not too unlike what they had been a hundred years ago. Many people died in their own beds or went to the hospital only to die. To go to the hospital was fearsome for that reason. Since death occurred in the home, the funerals were often built around the home too.

The deceased's body lay in state in the parlor, with the casket open for viewing, while relatives gathered around awkward in their best clothes and either sitting in the room with the body or standing in clumps in the yard. Children played outside and were shushed from time to time if they grew too loud, while the talk inside turned to praise of the deceased.

She was such a good person. To die while so young. The Lord took her. We will miss her. But the worst of all was "Doesn't she look natural?"

Hell, no. Not to me. She didn't look natural. She looked dead.

Dead! And I was scared out of my wits. No praise of the undertaker's cosmetic artistry made her look any less scary to me. She was dead. I didn't understand it. I didn't like it and I didn't want to be around the dead. I was a child facing something I didn't understand.

Picture the scene. Only thank God that my parents never put me through it, common as it was. The family entered the parlor where Aunt Dolly or Aunt Fanny lay in her coffin. Women dabbed their eyes with handkerchiefs. People talked in respectful tones. The visitors walked to the casket and stared down, respectfully admiring the undertaker's work. Laugh lines and age lines were smoothed out, too much cosmetic was applied. The hands were folded across the stomach and the room was unbearably warm, smelling of "pinks" or carnations from the garden, with their heavy odor being almost nauseating. A parent would pick up the child to look at dear Aunt Fanny. "Say goodbye to Aunt Fanny, dear." The child would recoil in fear or suck it's thumb. Some parents would even try to get the child to kiss Aunt Fanny goodbye. The child would scream and pull back while the parents were embarrassed. It was horrible. I always thought the child should wet his pants at that moment just to emphasize the point.

We gathered mainly for funerals and I hated them unlike anything since. Aunt Fanny, a school teacher, had banged her "limb" on a school desk corner, causing a permanent injury, and died. I couldn't understand it as a child but I still remember the stench of carnations in the living room. For nearly forty years of my adult life I have gardened and grown many flowers but because of these experiences I have never liked the "pink" or the carnation and would not grow them. That's conditioning!

Perhaps I should explain that the family always referred to Fanny's injury on her "limb" because the words "leg" or "thigh" were too personal to use, in too bad taste. Perhaps they even called the leg of a table or chair the "limb."

Such experiences as this funeral practice, which was followed by services in the church and also at the cemetery, definitely affected me today, as they probably have affected others. I abhor such services and will avoid going to a review as I avoid drinking poison. If necessary, I will slip into a funeral chapel to sign a visitor's register, and then leave. To me any holdover of funerals as I witnessed them as a boy is so archaic as to be medieval, tortuous to those left behind and an invasion of privacy to the dead. Memorial services with no casket, with no viewing, are about all I can stand, preferring to remember the dead as I knew them as living people.

Recently a friend told me that in her youth, living in a rural area, photographs were routinely taken of the dead in their casket and displayed on the mantels of the living rooms, sometimes for years.

No one will look down on me and say, "Doesn't he look natural?" How the hell would they know? The never saw me dead before.

Why I Hate War

I hate war because of what it did to Uncle Seb's feet.

But before getting into that, let me say how much fun it always was to visit on the farm at Uncle Seb and Aunt Flora's. I had been named after William Seborn Hull, my dad's brother, and this wonderful couple, without children of their own, welcomed me as an equal without the usual condescending attitude adults have for children.

Uncle Seb ran a small sawmill that had once been his Uncle Neil's. The house was built atop a hill overlooking the Lamine river upon whose banks was the sawmill, an adjoining shed or two, one of which was a cow barn. And down the private road, where a kid could run his bare feet through the hot summer dust, was Uncle Arth's house, also on the banks of the Lamine.

Seb also ran the community or family threshing machine, although I don't know who actually owned it; probably he did. He had a great warm laugh and on his shoulders was the mantle of a veteran. He had fought in the Great War, the War to End All Wars. Of course I liked him.

I had great fun at their house which was surrounded by fruit trees and rose bushes, including one I identified thirty years later as being Tausendschon. Geese in the chicken yard made me run like mad to and fro the outhouse and Seb even had a cream separator. What fun and magic it was to pour in whole milk, to turn the handle carefully at just the right speed and to see two types of liquid spill out the funnels. From one came the rich, heavy cream and from the other came the anemic skim milk.

Uncle Seb always had something going on, which is probably one reason I liked to go there. Once I even walked the seven miles there and seven more back to Madison to pass my Boy Scout fourteen-mile hike requirement.

Then there was the year the watermelon seed sprouted in the back yard near the pump. It was one of those drought years and Aunt Flora carefully saved her very scarce dishwater, carried it to the back door and watered the seedling melon vine. All summer she did this with tender, loving care until finally the day came when we could eat it. Alas, it tasted of soap so badly we had to feed it to the chickens, which would eat anything. That, in turn, is probably exactly the reason chicken yard eggs can't be sold on the market anymore.

Mornings on the farm were always glorious for a ten year old. As I look back it seemed I was always ten years old, because so many memories seem to be locked into that period.

We'd have a big farm breakfast and then Uncle Seb and I would head down the hill to the cattle. Sometimes we would go before breakfast. But the cows needed to be milked and fed and work needed to be done. The grass in the field was always high and wet with dew. The path was narrow so I always followed. Besides, there were apt to be snakes and Uncle Seb with his knee high rubber boots cleared away any imagined or actual obstacles and knocked down the grass for me to follow. It seemed that he knew just where to step to keep fairly dry and I tried to step in those same footsteps to avoid getting wet up to my knees. It didn't work too well. He was a man and I was a boy. Even worse was what the army had done to his feet. He walked with his toes pointed so far outwards that I couldn't match that angle. No matter how much I tried I looked deformed and the strain hurt my knees as I tried to turn the feet at least to a 45 degree angle. Ask any one of the few remaining World War I veterans. They'll tell you how the army forced country boys to walk at such extreme angles, all of those poor, displaced good ol' boys.

So, of course I hated war. I hated the English (my own ancestors), the French, and the Germans most of all because they got us into that crazy war that ruined Uncle Seb's feet. Thus I learned to hate war at an early age and haven't changed in all these years—except the reasons today make more sense to an adult mind.

You'll Break Your Damned Fool Neck

I remember my Dad telling me that Grandfather had said that to Uncle Pat once because Pat (Dad's youngest brother) drove like a whirlwind. And just to prove the point, he actually did break his neck.

To me, Pat was a hero, not because he rattled his spinal cord, but because he was a handsome man and an idol.

He should be pictured racing across the countryside in a Stutz Bearcat but he surely couldn't have afforded that stud car even if it had been available at that point in time. It was more apt to be a Chevrolet touring car which brought Pat to his near demise that day in 1924, when I was a wee lad of six.

Pat was undoubtedly what they called a high-spirited man. I'm sure he attended all the town baseball games held in Harley park where Madison's local team vied against teams from Rocheport and maybe even Columbia and Sedalia. Pat just had to be there with other guys, probably smoking Domino cigarettes and maybe accepting a swig from someone's bottle.

It seems to me that I just described many people's idea of a Good Ol' Boy.

Part of his ego was that he liked to drive fast. Not rapidly. Fast, like wide open. Like all out. Whatever the car would do Pat wanted to drive it at that speed.

Well, one day he did. He was driving out old original U.S. 40, came to a spot where it turned left and met a dirt

road coming in from the right. Directly out in front of him pulled that farmer with a load of hay, they tell me, and Pat had no choice but to plow directly into the wagon. Result: one broken neck.

That explained why Pat had such an erect neck the rest of his life. We kids noticed that but didn't really know the reason.

Around town this man I visualize as a gay young blade was seen by others. Mary Settles remembers seeing him with a cast on his neck but he was just another guy for a time, until a couple of years later they started dating and then were married in 1926.

That auto accident was one of two major dramatic events in Pat's life. The other was when he was 71 years old and doing a good turn for a sister-in-law, cleaning leaves from her gutters; he fell from the ladder to his death.

In retrospect he probably never once regretting driving all out, pedal to the metal, shoot the moon.

Maybe that daredevil part of him was what made us kids like him so much. Who knows?

Edgar Allan Poe's Cellar

When I grew older and started reading Edgar Allan Poe, I knew the exact location where those horrible crimes had been committed.

That had been in our cellar underneath our bedroom.

The McRoberts street house was a comfortable home, a soothing place for an afternoon nap or a long night's sleep. It was made so by a loving mother, always cooking delectables and smelling like fresh bread.

Also due to a hard working father, home from making a living, usually exhausted from that demanding job, but a man trying to be attentive to his boys.

I knew that cellar. I was sent there on occasion. The entrance was through a trap door on the back porch. One simply pulled up the ring on the floor and there under the door were the hidden stairs down into the dungeon—the cellar. Down there were kept home-canned vegetables, spiders, some coal, and, behind a bricked wall had to be the remains of Fortunato, the person imprisoned in THE CASK OF AMON-TILLADO. In the center of the room was an ancient and dusty table, which had a dark stain covering the surface. Probably blood. In fact, I knew without a doubt it was the place where the horrors of THE PIT AND THE PENDULUM had occurred.

I never did like that cellar.

I knew!

When mother asked me to fetch a jar of green beans or

jelly I was so scared I could barely lift the heavy door. I descended cautiously into that gloomy hole, lighted only by a twenty watt pendant light bulb. The spider webs in my face didn't help any either.

Was electricity so expensive or so new that it was not to be wasted? Were twenty watt bulbs that common? Or was it simply that my parents had lived on the farm where the only light was the dim glow of a coal oil lamp, which was considered sufficient?

Anyway, all those Poe stories had to have been written after Poe had visited our cellar.

Where Are You Now, Allan?

It was a long time ago, perhaps as long as sixty-five years ago, because I'm now an old man by some people's yardstick, and this happened when I was no older than eight.

It was a fun time for children to be growing up. The world had escaped from World War I and men like Uncle Seb had returned safely from the threat of the Kaiser. Times were good financially, although we kids had no knowledge of that. The depression was still a few years away and God was in His heaven.

The Fourth of July (nobody called it anything else) came on a hot, summer day and we kids were all set for an exciting time. In those olden days we had plenty of firecrackers, spit-dogs, all sorts of smaller explosives, including a few that could blow a tomato can twenty feet into the air.

Recently while driving through the south we noticed fireworks for sale in many states, huge roadside signs tempting us to stop. As dangerous as they are, and were many years ago, the boy in me wanted some of them. I recalled with joy stepping on those spit-dogs, or were they called hot-dogs? They popped and sputtered, breaking into pieces when stepped on. The joy was finding another small piece on the sidewalk and grinding it with the sole of your shoe until it exploded with a bang. And there were those round balls, big as a large marbles, which exploded beautifully when lobbed from a sling-shot up into the air and dropped on the street. Or when

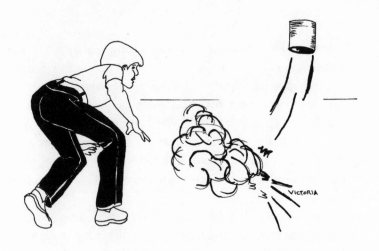

aimed flat out at a brick wall. They were great, but many children were hurt seriously with them.

There was Archie, an older boy, the only one with any sense, Allan, me, and the Johnson kids. Allan was the problem. He was a year or two older than me.

There was a new sidewalk in front of the Robertson house, which made it a fine smooth place to play—to ride my tricycle, which I was doing when I rode up to Allan. Now this wasn't a planned face-off, just an incident. He had been given a twenty-two pistol (probably like a starter's pistol in sports) and had it with him that day, just looking for something to shoot. I became that target. As I approached him he raised the pistol and pointed it straight at my face, five feet away, and pulled the trigger. The bullet hit me right in the face and killed me instantly.

No! No! That's not true. His cartridges were blanks. The paper load and the burned powder struck me directly in the face, just as I blinked. It was a hell of a shock if an eight year old could have said that. Of course my folks rushed me to Doctors Beckett and Stone.

The burnt powder was imbedded in my face and eyelids, causing the doctor to spend considerable time trying to pick out the black spots from my skin. He commented how lucky it was that I blinked because otherwise I would have lost my sight. After some time of my complaints and his impatience, he gave up, saying that they would heal over.

I don't know what ever happened to Allan. Was he punished? Was the pistol confiscated by his parents? I don't know. But, Allan, wherever you are, I hope we meet again because I owe you one.

Before Moving

But before we moved from McRoberts street there were the days of infancy and boyhood.

Oh, for the fun we had. There was the experience of having been born at home—a home previous to McRoberts street. I never remembered anything about the birth of course, but my parents told me all the details. It was of another time and place with fewer doctors, home births being the common event. Sometimes a doctor was present. Sometimes not.

As I say when pushed to tell of my family, "I was one of seven children—all beautiful kids." Then I will admit that I was really only one of two, but by my eighth birthday I was one of one. However, that's another story I've already told.

There were the Howells, the Mustangs, the Humpfeldts, and others but I and my brother Charles, two years my senior, played with them all and had many friends. We played all the kid games. "Alley Oop," our version of throwing the ball over the house, tag games which were particularly fun when it was getting dark and parents were permitting a few extra minutes before bedtime. Of course there was much yelling and running, which was the prime fun of all, followed by the bedtime bath, a real necessity by that time.

"But, oh, those baked potatoes." I remember. The older boys showed us how to do it. First, we built a fairly good sized fire on a bare spot in the empty lot, two houses away, and hoped the scrap wood was sufficient to make some good coals. As a rule, it was mere kindling and burned up too quickly. A boy took his potato, made some mud in the lot and plastered the unpeeled potato with a coating of mud. Then it was either just laid in the coals or placed in an empty tin can and slipped into the fire. Although it required about an hour to cook, we usually gave up about the time the mud coating was scalding hot, and then pulled our potato from the fire or from the can. The mud was knocked off, only to find the potato still raw, perhaps burned on the outside, but very hot. The smart boys threw away the potatoes but there weren't very many smart ones. As I said, "Mostly we ate the burned, hot, dirty potatoes, or as much as we could stand, then bragged about how good they were. We dubbed the recipe either 'Mudpotatoes' or 'Potato in a can'."

Life was neither simple nor boring.

There were other things happening too. This neighborhood was at the edge of town on a hill which sloped in several directions. The most interesting direction was down toward the railroad tracks. It was fun to go down there, probably two blocks distance, unbeknownst to our parents and place pennies on the tracks, then to await the passing of a heavy Katy (Missouri, Kansas and Texas) or a Missouri Pacific train. After the train was gone we would try to locate our pennies, some of which had flown away from the tracks, some remaining exactly where placed.

But the tracks were more interesting when the circus came to town. People who never lived in a small town, who never saw a circus train unload, couldn't possibly have known the real excitement of the circus.

The train always seemed to creep into town during the night and then next morning there it would be. We kids rushed down to where we could sit on the bank and see the animals. The huge elephants helping to unload crates and wagons containing other animals, like the lions, the tigers.

The elephants helped the big draft horses move wagons full of tents and supplies, all very impressive to little kids who had never seen any animal bigger than a farm horse or a cow in the country.

And, of course, there was a parade. Eventually it reached Main street, with its line of elephants each holding the preceding one's tail and swinging heavy footed down the street, while a steam calliope in a wagon played its screeching melody. "Boy," I thought recently, "How I'd like my grandchildren to have a chance to see a real live circus parading down the main streets of a small American town. It's just not the same as seeing them on television, or in a circus amphitheatre, or even visiting a circus wagon museum where so many beautiful wagons are preserved."

Miss Martinetti

The first year at any school is dramatic—whether it's junior high, college, or graduate school. In each case it's a new experience, with many lessons of deportment and procedure to be learned.

So was grade school.

Picture this wimpy little boy of six or seven walking to his first year of school, to the end of McRoberts street, left down another street one block long, to Spring street where I turned right, continuing downhill past the mulberry tree, a corner grocery, the Schrack-Givens grocery warehouse, near the ice company, across the first set of dangerous train tracks, soon the second set of tracks, past the grain elevator and the hatchery and up the long hill, eventually leading to Main street.

(Sad to relate, on a recent trip to Madison I found the sets of tracks gone, removed when train service left the town, the tracks being replaced by a walking/biking trail for many miles. The elevator, gone. The hatchery, gone—all of that memorabilia gone.)

Then right on Main street in the very heart of town, down many blocks, past the high school, the telephone company's new brick building all the way to turn left one block to the school. "Central School" that is. The grade school.

It was a very long one and one-tenth miles as measured recently but to a little kid's memory it seemed like eight miles.

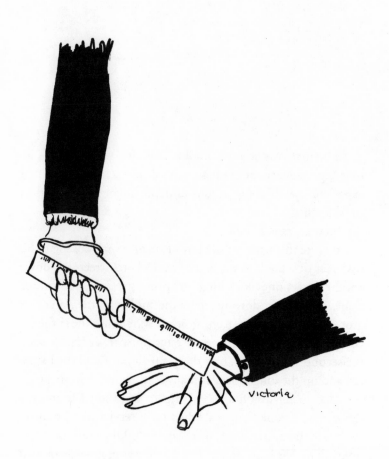

victoria

Central school was a two or three story brick building, not replaced, because of a fire I think. The fire theory seems reasonable because I recall bare wood floors, treated heavily with oil, as was the custom in those days, thus making the floors very flammable.

I can't remember this particular teacher's name but it should have been Martinetti which would have been very descriptive.

Miss Martinetti was elderly. Gray hair in a bun to a child of six equates "old" and that was the picture I retained these long years. But there were some things I can't forget about her. She apparently was determined to teach her children by keeping them scared to death.

Her weapon was a ruler, which never left her hand. As we studied, or read, she patrolled the aisles, towering over her small charges.

"Whack!" Down would come the ruler on some poor kid's knuckles—maybe even on the back of the skull.

"Whack!" Another kid, half dozing, was awakened.

"Whack!" A little blond girl got a knuckle rap.

"Whack!" A burly overweight boy got it on the tender back of the skull.

"Turn you hand over" she said and a kid did so, palm up.

"Whack!" went the ruler on the flat palm, stinging mercilessly, while the kid cried quietly.

This kind of teaching would surely not be permitted today. Parents and teachers would cause it to be stopped. Or a gun-toting kid would take action. God forbid!

Imagine what would have happened in a school of the nineteen-twenties had a seven-year-old-child brought a loaded pistol to school. The teacher would have run from the room screaming and wetting her underpants. The principal would have called the police to take the kid away, and the superintendent would have tried the local version of stump-hanging as Indians in Washington state reportedly did to prisoners. (Details on request.)

Of course there were no food programs. We bought our own meager lunches from home and ate them on playground breaks, while the teachers honed their rulers and spit fire inside the building.

This is out of character for me to attack a teacher, whom I'm certain was a lone character, not typical. My wife and I were both teachers with Master's degrees; our first born daughter is teacher/manager of a Montessori pre-school unit; her dearest cousin is an elementary teacher. None of these people would possibly act like Miss Martinetti did.

A question. Why did parents permit this practice by an individual teacher? Surely they knew of her ruler-wielding. Was it because they believed in the practice of sparing the rod, spoiling the child? I doubt it. The parents I knew were loving, kindly people who believed there was no place for cruelty in child raising.

Dust Between the Toes

Have you ever played in the dust? In the dirt?

Have you ever sat down in the summer and scooped and scraped the dirt until you could shovel or spoon it into a toy truck? There's a certain pleasure in this because a child can play with it and not think of it in terms of "dirt." It's just sun-warmed dust to be played with in loading a small dump truck or to walk through briefly, barefooted, while feeling the dry warm dust squish up between the toes.

That's the boy's treatment of the situation.

The girl's treatment requires water. She has to have water to add to the dust to create mud. That's because she can't make mudpies unless they can be shaped into patties, as they've seen their mothers make patty cake hamburgers or patty cake pancakes.

Don't stop the kids from these simple pleasures. Usually no harm is done. Dust comes away with a hand dusting of clothing and mud dries and disappears.

Didn't you ever make patty cakes or feel the warm dust squish up between your toes?

It's much better than playing in the sand box which the neighborhood cats visit every night.

Watching a Hanging

Public executions were not everyday experiences in the days of my boyhood. There had been one in 1891 of a man who had killed a vagrant, again in 1901 of a man nicknamed Jocko who had killed the town marshall, one of a man named Reeves (first name either Charles or Spinner) and not another until January 31, 1930.

That's the one I "saw"—on January 31, 1930 when they executed Lawrence Mabrey (aka Mabry), a youth found guilty of a murder in Sedalia and, on a change of venue, tried, sentenced and hanged in Madison.

There is a great deal of confusion in my mind about this execution. I've researched it through the Friends of Madison and the Missouri State Historical Society in Columbia but am still dissatisfied.

The problem is that I distinctly remember looking out of a window of the sheriff's family quarters at the county jail and witnessing the turmoil of people in the yard at the rear of the jail, the crowd focusing on the old barn in which the hanging was proceeding. This seems a conflict of possibilities because I would have been in that residential part of the jail only during 1920–1924 when I was only 2 to 6 years of age, at a time when my grandfather, Charles Hull, was county sheriff and lived there with his family. Then I learn that the only hanging not occurring in the yard but in the barn was

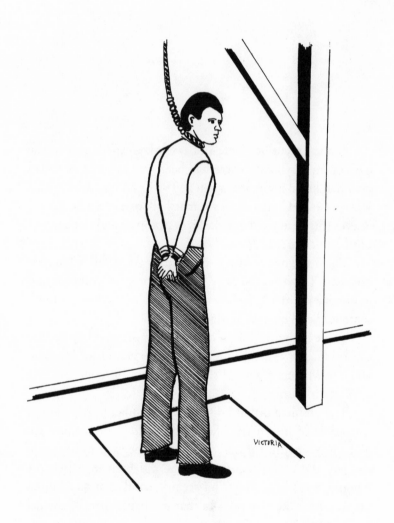

that of Mabrey in 1930 when I was twelve years old and Granddad no longer sheriff.

The key question is, since it is obvious that I must have witnessed part of the scene in 1930, when I had no access to the sheriff's living quarters, my grandfather was no longer sheriff—the new man being Clay Groom.

Anyway, I was there because I remember the huge crowd of people in the rear jail yard and all of the excitement as Mabrey was hanged in the loft of the old barn instead of on an open gallows in the yard.

Of course the event was traumatic to me, regardless of my age. I pictured my grandfather actually killing this bad man, whereas he only had to make the arrangements. He was fifty years my senior and whether it was he or Clay Groom who presided at the execution, he was obeying orders of the court which found Mabrey guilty. Although Granddad was a big man, and elected to his position by a landslide, he was not cruel. Never once did I hear of him being cruel to any person, black or white.

The only official record I can find of the event was in the words of Elston J. Melton, local newspaper publisher/reporter and author, who witnessed the execution and who wrote:

"Mabrey maintained that he was innocent. Hunched in harness, he faced reporters and officials in a barn loft behind the county jail on a bitter cold Friday morning, January 31, 1930, and made a long, rambling statement while multitudes outside the jail yard bought execution 'extras' describing his death and arrival of the hearse, before either had materialized. Otherwise, everything went as per schedule and the imported hangman later declared 'That was the nicest execution I ever handled.'"*

I still wonder how I got past everyone and had a chance to overlook some of those events.

---

*"Melton's History," by E. J. Melton, © 1937.

Christmas Fires

At this moment we're not talking about roaring fires in fireplaces on Christmas eve while people struggle inside from the new-fallen snow.

No. We're talking about fires that burned down houses in the days before electricity, particularly in rural areas.

All because of candles on Christmas trees.

That may sound ridiculous to modern young people but in the days before electricity came down the road to farmhouses, people placed candles on their decorated Christmas trees to provide illumination and that beautiful seasonal aura. The problem was that it was also a very dangerous process, causing many a tree to burst into flame and people to rush outdoors to see their beloved house burn to the ground.

But some of us remember that lovely soft light and foolishly like to experience it again. As adults, Carol and I wanted to relive that experience, so we set about trying to locate the candles and holders.

Not an easy job until we learned of a store in Minneapolis, called J. D. Holtzermann, Inc., located then at 417–423 Cedar Avenue. Holtzermann's sold food, wines, some clothing but its true magnificence was its collection of German handblown Christmas tree ornaments. The basement part of the store was a wonderbar of these glorious ornaments. Oh, how we wished we could afford to buy lots of them—but we couldn't.

VICTORIA

But we did locate, of all things, old-fashioned clip-on candle holders and candles to fit into them. Those candles were about three or four inches high and twisted.

Sure we used them, being young and foolish and wanting our young children to experience that same glee we remembered. We had a second tree in our basement amusement room, to which we clipped the unique candle holders, complete with candles.

Of course we burned the house down.

Not true! Not true! But we gathered around and admired the beautiful glow while father Billy Boy stood nearby with two large buckets full of water and an all-purpose fire extinguisher. Believe me, we admired the tree for a few minutes then quickly extinguished each lighted candle, never to use them again.

But another generation got to see a candle-lighted Christmas tree.

The Penny

Did you ever have one of those flattened copper pennies from a carnival? They were a unique thing and cost us kids more than a penny, but we were proud owners.

We also found a way to make our own.

When we lived on McRoberts street we walked down the hill a block or so to the railroad tracks, where we'd lie in wait for the afternoon train.

"I can hear it coming!" Carl Wilhite would yell.

"Then shut up and let's get going," someone else would reply. Then we'd run down the bank to put our pennies in a row on the track. Someone might even gamble a nickel, but pennies seemed to work better.

Then we'd climb back up the clay side of the hill to be safely away from the train which would now be upon us.

It would whistle like mad for the crossing a half mile or so beyond us; usually it didn't stop but was steaming and roaring, crashing down upon us with such noise that we covered our ears to avoid the pain. I'm sure the engineer would remember that crazy kid (not me) who had tried to sled down the street hill and make his way under the moving train cars with their crashing wheels.

The pennies usually stayed there while the engine and coal car and up to a hundred heavily loaded freight cars followed along, each wheel further flattening our coins. Sometimes a penny would go zinging past us into the weeds but

Victoria

times a penny would go zinging past us into the weeds but most of them either stayed atop the rail or dropped alongside.

When the train was gone, we'd rush down to reclaim our booty. We'd each usually find two or three and claim them as our own, fully recognizing that no one could challenge us with any hope of success.

They truly were flattened, sometimes being slightly curved if they worked their way to the edge of the rail. Now we could brag about what we were going to do with them. The most impressive claim was that we were going to engrave the Pledge of Allegiance on each penny, just as the carny guys did.

Of course we were going to do that!

Light Bread

When I was a "wee cowrin', timorous beastie"* my mother would sometimes say to me, "Billy Boy, don't eat candy or raisins this afternoon because we are going to have fresh lightbread for dinner." Or when we visited great aunt Bess, my grandfather Hull's sister-in-law, she would have just baked bread—no, not "bread" but "lightbread."

The use of that term has concerned me mightily; I've discussed it with many people, tried to research it and have decided it was a regional term, completely unknown to the Scandinavians in Minnesota where I now live. Huge milling firms to whom I have written either don't reply at all or have no knowledge of the source of the term.

I kept asking myself and others: Was it a term that developed because housewives now had a finely ground flour, much superior to what they had used before? Was it about the time a big national firm marketed a soft, live baking yeast for the first time? Was it a welcome relief from either cornbread or biscuits? Whatever caused the introduction of the term, it must have been a mighty event. Apparently while the rest of the world called it "bread" those people in a small portion of the midwest called it "lightbread."

Lois Kemp, an employee of a large Twin City grocery chain, remembers that "lightbread" was the term also used in western Kentucky, really not too far from Missouri. Ms.

Kemp also thought it possible that the term referred to commercially baked, sliced and wrapped bread.

William E. Lockhart, Ph.D., American Institute of Baking, Manhattan, Kansas, seems to agree with Ms. Kemp. He says he "used to hear the term 'lightbread' in the 1930s in Linn county, Kansas, a county adjacent to the Missouri border." "Lightbread," he continued, "was used to describe yeast-raised white bread in comparison to cornbread or quickbread such as biscuits."**

In any event, it was a welcomed bit of food. Few things can equal a piece of freshly baked bread, or lightbread, still warm, with homemade country sweet cream butter spread on it. Oh, my diet!

---

*Robert Burns.

** Letter of May 17, 1993.

Crack Away, Lord

At first, as a small boy, I probably regarded Jesus with a mixture of respect and fear but, eventually, learned to love Him as my Lord.

My mother was undoubtedly the most sincere Christian human being in the world. She knew! She believed! She practiced! She showed respect.

In those days there was an expression in common use, probably most often said during an electrical storm. People would jump with astonishment at a very strong bolt of lightning and the loud clap of thunder.

"Boy, that hit something nearby."

"Look outside to see if there's a tree down."

"Crack away, Lord."

I think it was an expression of bravado, somewhat of fear, certainly not challenging God to send us a bolt of lightning. Maybe it was said out of context, meaning even admiration, such as "Lord, I know you are showing us your great power and that, if you wished to do so, you could crack away and explode anything or any person you wanted to."

I can't remember any specific person saying "Crack away, Lord" but I heard it frequently. It's just the sort of thing a kid would repeat in a repeat situation, but had brother Charles or I used it, we would have been corrected very quickly.

Once, during such a storm, when I was under eight, we were having an electrical storm. We weren't struck but we received a shock. Mother and I were sitting on the edge of an iron bed, me on mother's lap, when suddenly we experienced such a tingle that we both cried out as we could see the iron head and footboards emitting sparks. That's all, but I've remembered it a lifetime.

That was nothing compared with what happened over sixty years later. Wife Carol and I were watching television in a den at the rear of our house, during a summer thunderstorm. BLAM, we thought an atom bomb had exploded, but it was lightning hitting a maple tree twenty-five feet from us. It split that tree in half, dropping half on a metal fence to the north, the juice following that fence to the west near the house, following a closed gate and hitting the house with such power that it blew a hole in the side of the house (the dining room). Then it went throughout the entire house wiring. It destroyed four light bulbs in an overhead fixture in a bedroom and exploded the new Sanyo television we were watching.

It would have been a good time to say, "Lord, you really cracked away then," but I can assure you we were more interested in saying, "What the hell happened?"

I can remember saying, "If I were only younger I would have run out there and opened that gate so the electricity couldn't have crossed it to the house."

Sure I would have.

Boyhood Years

Spring Street Blues

As I've said, we lived my first eight years on McRoberts street, which was a short little side street off Spring, a major street that ran all the way from one end of town to the other.

Now Spring street—ah, that was a street. It started for many of us at Harley park, but actually ran beyond it for a ways, and went down a long hill, across the railroad tracks, past the old elevator and headed for Main street, where the J. C. Penney store eventually occupied one corner and the bank the other.

It was a street that figured in my childhood in several events. We even lived on it for a while on the downward side of the hill, before the flatland wherein lay the tracks.

Halfway down that hill, where we lived in a rented house, owned by a family named something like Holtz, but just across the street was a fine big mulberry tree. If you've never sat in a mulberry tree, stuffing your face with those sweet, ripe purple fruit, you haven't lived. Of course we practically fought off the birds who liked the fruit too, with its luscious purple juices. Those purple juices caused lots of concern to our mothers because they created a stain hard to remove from our clothes.

That hill also almost figured in a couple of accidents. Hazel Johnson was a brave lad a few years older than I and liked to ride his sled down this paved street in the winter, going full blast down toward the railroad tracks. You guessed it—one time when he approached the tracks there was a slow moving train crossing Spring street. At that very spot some of us kids figured Hazel was a goner, but he made it, barely missing one set of wheels on a boxcar and getting through before the second set reached him. If he didn't wet his pants he probably was the only one of the gang because I'm sure most of us were scared for him.

Years previously, that hill had also nearly been the end of my dad. When I reached middle age and started riding motorcycles, my dad confided in me that he had once owned an Indian. That was a very popular cycle in those days. He had been going down that same Spring street hill and, while crossing the first set of tracks, the bike skittered away from him and slammed into the brick building of Schrack-Givens grocery warehouse. That's about all he would tell me but I'm sure he had a very unhappy occasion.

Then it became my turn. Hazel and my dad had their experiences, but so did I. When we were living on McRoberts street, I traveled down that hill to go to school, being no more than eight years old. One miserable, cold winter day when there had been an ice storm, I was climbing the far hill, past the elevator, on the slippery sidewalk, when WHAM my feet flew out from under me and I went down like the proverbial load of rock. I hit hard, felt hurt, probably cried some and went on to school. Later it was discovered I had a hernia and had to wear a truss, a most uncomfortable and embarrassing device.

About two years later, at age ten, the hernia was repaired surgically when undergoing an emergency appendectomy.

So Spring street and I have lots of memories. It's too bad that I can't recall some good events, some happy events, that occurred on Spring street. Oh, yes, let's not forget that Hazel made it safely and we kids annually had our fill of mulberries.

Evelyn's Birth

I well remember the night cousin Evelyn was born. Uncle Pat and Aunt Mary lived further up the street on McRoberts, and Mary was pregnant for the first time. I recall being with my dad, with Pat and a group of other family men, down the street and around the corner in someone else's home, while Mary was in labor up the street.

It was a new experience for me, being just a kid and not knowing anything about where babies came from. The men sat around and played cards all evening and probably lifted a glass of bourbon from time to time. All I did was learn to play solitaire until I fell asleep. Eventually I was told that I had a new cousin, that Evelyn Jane had been born.

At the time I probably thought, so what? I have enough cousins now and this one is a girl!

Swimming in Rotten Egg Water

In the county there was a famous park known as Chouteau Springs, closed these days but just off Interstate I-70.

It was privately owned but came into being because the French explorer, Pierre Chouteau, bargained there with the Osage Indians. This was during times when Daniel Boone and his sons were establishing salt licks in nearby Howard and Boone counties of Missouri.*

Chouteau Springs must have been in its heyday before my time. Perhaps the twenties, maybe earlier. By the thirties when we Boy Scouts and Sunday School groups went to Chouteau there were no longer signs of the rip-roaring dances and parties held there during my parents' years. Then there had been good country dances, some good illegal alcohol products, and good music.

To us, it was a place to swim and to cavort. Many of us will long remember that magnificent Sunday school teacher, James Wooldridge Farris, who took us there repeatedly for outings. We knew him as "Mr. Jim." He was a fine man but probably a little too nice, a little too effete to be a Good Ol' Boy. Maybe too much of a gentleman.

But the most memorable part of the event was the terrible stench of the water. It was usually described as smelling like rotten eggs and supposedly had great curative powers. People came to take it home in large containers, or to swill it

VICTORIA

down while there. It really made itself known, whether you smelled it, drank it, or swam in it. One of its curative powers was that it became a purgative which only meant it was fun to talk some newcomer boy into drinking it, then later watch him suddenly run for the bushes. We were mean.

Recently I drove off I-70, which replaced US 40, to drive over the flinty hills to find old Chouteau closed, barricaded and awaiting a new entrepreneur to sink a bundle and open a new spa. A few million would do it.

---

*"Melton's History," by E. J. Melton, E. W. Stephens Publishing Company, Columbia, Missouri, © 1937, page 20.

Grandparents' House

My paternal grandparents, Charlie and Lillian Hull, lived in a little white frame house located between the village of Lamine, Missouri, and the nearby Lamine river. Originally highway 41 had run directly before the front yard but then the highway was moved back a block or so and paved. going past their house it had forded the Lamine river, now having left its abutments there to attract fisherfolks and wandering children. Nearby was the new steel and concrete bridge and the "new 41." We had to walk a plank to cross over the ditch in front of my grandparents' house, that ditch being the only remains of "old 41." The house was basically a four-room, two-porch square, probably built about ought ten or ought fourteen.

From the front, two porches were visible, at both the left and right ends of the building, the intervening section being part of the parlor. The larger porch was at the left and featured the main entrance door to the house. On that porch hung a chain suspended swing like millions of others over the country; it was a good place to loaf an hour away.

That front porch was the imagined setting of a yarn I heard years later. The story concerned a man teaching trust to his boy child. He placed his son on the railing and stood below him on the narrow concrete walk leading around the house to the rear door. "Jump," he exclaimed to his son. "Come on, son, jump and I'll catch you. Trust me. Jump!"

The boy simply had to have faith in his own father, so eventually he did jump. Just as the father was about to break the boy's fall, he stepped back so the boy could go splat on the concrete walk. While the child cried and screamed at his father, the dad said to him "Let that be a lesson to you. Don't ever trust anyone. No one! Do you hear me. Trust no one."

Entering the house, one was immediately in the living room with a double bed against the far wall. It was a combination sitting room and spare bedroom.

The room was dominated by a beautiful seven foot tall, three foot wide hall tree, of lovely oak. It featured a large, beveled mirror and four brass clothes hooks shaped like deer racks. It had a rather low seat with arms on each side; the seat flipped up and we children were instructed to remove our shoes and place them in the bin below the lid. This lovely old piece of furniture eventually became mine, having been passed down to oldest son (my father Aubrey) and then again to oldest grandchild (me). I refinished it and kept it in our house for many years until very recently when space and fire worries convinced me to dispose of it to a dealer, where it was greatly appreciated. It was in excess of a hundred years old.

That sitting room also contained a wood heating stove, a small oak table, grandfather's rolltop desk, a couple of rocking chairs and a mantle. No fireplace, just a mantle as a shelf to hold a fine old clock. It was black onyx and chimed beautifully even at the quarter hour. How badly I wanted that clock in the future but when grandfather died, having been preceded in death by grandmother, I was away, probably at college, and missed my chance to get the clock. It was my understanding it was to be mine but I could never remember whether that had been a promise from grandfather or an assumption by me. Anyway it went to my Aunt Geneva, who had a more legitimate claim to it anyway.

The stove was just another low-slung horizontal wood

burner which one had to dodge when passing into the adjoining kitchen.

That little oak table had been a mess until my mother stripped it of many layers of varnish. My father often commented that when he or one of his siblings obviously had idle hands about to get into trouble, grandmother made them varnish that table, so it gradually changed to a very dark color.

If we didn't go into the kitchen, we could go into the parlor, which occupied that part of the front of the house between the two porches. That room was not used for wakes for deceased family members, like was the custom of my mother's family in nearby Pilot Grove, Missouri. All it was to us was the room with the piano—more importantly, the piano stool. We skirmished to ride that revolving seat until one of us fell off and was hurt. Then we would play "Chopsticks".

In addition to the large iron cookstove, the kitchen contained a long table easily seating twelve adults. Around it were drawn these straight backed chairs, ancient already by the time I came into the family. They may have been my great-grandparents' chairs and possibly came overland from Winston Salem, North Carolina, by covered wagon years previously. They creaked and objected to body shifting: some were supported and tightened by wire stretched from leg to leg to seat, holding the chair together to avoid its collapse due to glue deterioration and loosening of legs and cross supports. But, oh, the glorious food we consumed while sitting on those chairs. But, of course, that experience was later on for us kids because there was no room for us at the table. We were placed at separate tables wherever there was room and fed generously. Being the eldest and largest grandchild, as well as being very sensitive, I often thought that feeding us was not too distant a procedure from slopping the hogs. I may have been more perceptive than I realized.

The only two remaining areas of the house were my grandparents' bedroom and the pantry.

The bedroom was at the far side of the house and was behind the second porch. It had a huge bed with a featherbed so deep I once thought I would smother and die in it. Usually it had a bottom-wet baby atop the bed and we were shushed if we even started to enter the sanctorum. "Don't wake up the baby."

At the rear of the house, also off the kitchen, was the pantry and rear entrance. Come to think of it, every room was off the kitchen, indeed the center of activity.

The pantry/back entryway had two pieces of furniture. The first was a kitchen cabinet, to use its proper nomenclature. It was a design so common that millions must have been in use for a hundred years or more in this country. It had a porcelain shelf in the center which pulled out to become a food preparation area. Space below was for pots and pans while the top right section provided space for food brought up from the cellar and spices. The upper left portion was the flour bin, which tapered down to a built in sifter under which a bowl could be placed. My grandmother probably made biscuits at that spot every morning of her life.

The other piece in this entry room was a table used for washing when one came in from barn or field. Atop it sat the usual wash pan, water pitcher, and soap. A roller towel hung nearby. The table itself was a marvelous piece; at least it is today after we rescued it from my father's barn and completely refinished it. It has turned walnut legs, walnut frame and a top of alternating pieces of walnut and white pine, creating a nice pattern. It had come from a pre-prohibition saloon in Madison and has a small built-in box at each corner, under the table top; there the card player could place his whiskey glass. Since the little shelf was open on two sides, there surely were episodes when a lefty sitting at the right of a

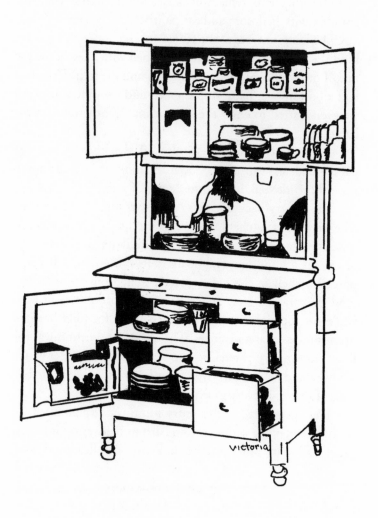

right-handed player accidentally reached into the wrong shelf.

Blacksnakes in the Tree

Uncle Seb and Aunt Flora had one of those yard swings with facing seats and an open floor footrest, in which you sat facing each other and swung back and forth.

It was a wonderful place to rest, there on the farm, with a cool drink of water or maybe a lemonade, sitting under that huge maple at the corner of their house.

We had been working doing something. That is Uncle Seb was working and I, just a small boy, tagged along to be in the way.

Upon a very hot day, we two were sitting there catching a stray bit of breeze and plop, plop something from overhead splashed down onto the swing, making a mess. We both looked up . . .

Uncle Seb yelled, "Get out of the way, Bill!" and we both scrambled off the swing.

He ran to the house and returned quickly with a twelve gauge shotgun, aimed it up into the tree and fired both barrels.

WHAM! I thought he'd sever the whole limb upon which the two big blacksnakes lay, but no, he only severed the snakes, which came crashing down onto the swing in segments.

I never again enjoyed sitting under that tree but, at that time, I was glad to have Uncle Seb, everybody's Good Ol' Boy, there to handle the situation.

VICTORIA

Victoria

The Biggest Mudcat

Want to make a bet? Before this story is told I'll tell you of the biggest mudcat I ever saw—but there'll be at least three people who'll say, "Oh, that's nothing. I know of a fellow who caught a bigger one."

Of course you know what a mudcat is. It has nothing to do with a Caterpillar tractor stuck in the mud or my daughter's twenty-five-pound cat when it got dirty—but that would have been a mess worth seeing.

A mudcat is a catfish, a very large catfish usually, caught in one of Missouri's rivers, whether it's the old Mizzou itself, the Mississippi, or one of the smaller tributaries like the Lamine, the Blackwater or the Osage.

But they grew big and the men who caught them had a handful just getting them ashore.

Mostly they seemed to be catching them on trotlines; a trotline is a series of hooks suspended on a long line distributed along a muddy river or creek, the drop lines being at intervals and the whole line sometimes supported at intervals with jugs. Sometimes they preferred to call the procedure "jugging."

For bait they differed drastically. One old fellow would say there was nothing as appealing to catfish as rotten chicken guts and another would insist that doughballs were by far the best. They were exactly what the name indicated, being balls of raw dough stuck onto hooks. I suppose every true fisherman had his own recipe, some to flavor the doughballs, others to leave them just plain and ordinary.

But they caught some whoppers. The biggest one I ever saw was in a photo in a newspaper (Truth!) It had been hauled to an open touring car, probably something like a model T Ford.

If there were a top, it was down and the fish lay on the floor behind the front seats. That ugly thing hung out the car on both sides. Yes, it was so long the snout extended on one side and the tail the other. The fisherman was proud to claim that it weighted over a hundred pounds. I believed it then and I do now.

On the other hand, my great Uncle Arth once caught one on the Lamine river that weighed a hundred and twelve, while my dad told me of a guy in Rocheport who caught one that weighed about a hundred and twenty.

I often wonder how much of those monsters were edible? Maybe they cut them in chunks and buried them in the cornfields as the early Indians taught us to do.

Of course it brands me as a heretic to say it, but I'd rather have a walleye anytime.

A Mile a Minute was Nothing

At one hundred miles an hour the gasoline truck roared down U.S. 40, a projectile from hell searching for something to smash into and become a hundred foot fireball.

It made the notorious mile-a-minute speed, so frequently talked about, seem like nothing.

It was illegal. It was dangerous. It was damned foolishness.

But no one told that to the driver, me, a fourteen-year-old kid who finally had his chance to drive alone.

It was my dad's gas truck, loaded to the gills with the good stuff, ready to be delivered to stations along U.S. 40. Today's memory doesn't recall how I happened to have the chance to drive, but the scene was now set.

Out onto 40 the truck rolled and the mph increased. Sixty was just cruising, seemingly nothing. Then came seventy, eighty, oh, hell, let's do it.

It barely made the one hundred mark.

But just as I reached one hundred, I came up behind an old couple in the family Essex. They and the Essex bounced two hundred feet and the gas truck did indeed burst into flames, incinerating me.

No! Not true! All lies!

But it could have happened except that old couple had sense enough to stay home that day.

The truck was permitted to decelerate and I eventually took it back home, no one being the wiser.

The next one hundred mph trip occurred about five years later when I was a passenger in Lloyd's car—Lloyd's father's car that is.

Lloyd wanted to show off (those awful words) what his dad's car could do on the Fayette road. It did one hundred, accompanied by the excited yelling of six young men.

Again, nothing terrible happened. That same old couple, now five years older, again had the good sense to stay off the highway. After all, who wants to get killed by six young idiots showing off?

Not six. Just five. The reader knows that I was the one telling Lloyd to slow down.

Sure I was.

What it Feels Like to Fail

Maybe this should be titled "What It's Like To Be A Sissy."

I wasn't noted as being strong and dominating. I tried and even bought the Charles Atlas course titled something like "How to Be Strong and Beat the Hell Out of Everybody." In fact I still have it buried deeply in a basement bookcase. But I still didn't develop the athletic figure I visualized.

Why? My father and paternal relatives were all masculine and strong but here I came along, the mixture of that blood and that of a lovely not-so-strong mother.

I caught every childhood disease that hit town. Mumps, chicken pox, scarlet fever, whooping cough, *ad infinitum,* even polio. Yes, damned if I didn't and it almost wiped me out.

I'd get over something and just about the time I regained my strength and vigor along came Double-Strength Pink Eye, Thirty-Seven Day Influenza, Or Lifetime Pneumonia. About the only thing I missed was smallpox and the black death. It was all punctuated by a birthday card an artist employee of my father sent me on my seventh or eighth birthday. It showed a rampaging English bulldog furiously chasing an infuriated black cat with hair raised. The caption read "Remember, Billy, Life is Just One Damned Thing After Another."

He was right.

But that didn't help me. While I did well scholastically and some considered me a brain (later I was admitted to Mensa), I was a washout as a jock.

I hated gym classes. Tall, scrawny, with a practically useless polio injured right arm, I couldn't do the required rope climb off the gym floor. The teacher was so crude and unsympathetic as to urge me to "try harder." I should have told him, "You damned fool. How do you think trying harder is going to help a one-armed kid?"

So I suffered. I embarrassed. I withered. All I could do was run track. The school provided no athletic equipment, such as track shoes, so my folks had to buy them by mail from Sears or Wards in Kansas City. No matter how much they cost my poor parents, they were cheap and inadequate. Their thin soles, with cleats attached over paper-thin leather soles, gave my poor feet no protection and I ran in great pain with metatarsal damage that lasted for years. No trained coach to supervise what was happening or to care about my inadequate equipment.

Somehow I lived through it without permanently damaging my arches. I eventually found tennis more to my liking, although it necessitated playing at six or seven in the morning, before the hot days of the thirties reached one hundred or more degrees.

Of course I grew up, became much stronger and, partly out of defense, found I was better suited to intellectual efforts than to athletic ones and gradually accepted my role in life.

It says here.

Marilyn's Bicycle

The Colonel and Mrs. Colonel lived across the street from us when I was about twelve. But, pardon me, I should say that our family lived in a rented house directly across the street from the Colonel and Mrs. Colonel.

They were good people. Nice people. Lovely people. As president of the prestigious military school, the Colonel and Mrs. Colonel lived in that lovely gray and white house.

Prestigious people. Monied people. Believe me, people on whom we neighborhood kids would not even think of playing Halloween tricks.

They were respected.

In those days the Colonel and Mrs. Colonel bought a new car almost every year as I remember it. It was always a big black car, imposing, powerful and beautiful. I think it was always a Packard. At that time no other auto challenged the prestige of the Packard.

And, of course, it was a stick shift because that's what all cars were in those early years.

I used to stand under the catalpa tree and watch with awe and envy as Mrs. Colonel would drive away from the front of the house in that big, beautiful black Packard. Sometimes I hid up in the tree.

She would get in the car, start the motor and rev it up until she could hear it quite well. It is assumed that she had diminished hearing because the car would reach the stage

where it was roaring at several thousand RPMs. Then, taking a good grip on the steering wheel, keeping the RPMs very high, she would suddenly let out the clutch. Now, young people today, with our automatic transmissions may not be able to picture what happened next.

So, you say, what happened?

The car would buck, spin its rear wheels while it tried to get a grip on the street paving, then shoot down the street as if it were going to reach sixty miles per hour in five seconds, tires screeching and smoking, until Mrs. Colonel let up on the accelerator and the car would slow down.

Then she would drive all over town at a very sedate speed of ten or fifteen miles per hour.

There were lots of activities on third street to keep me involved.

Perhaps nothing was more exciting that when I was permitted to ride a visiting girl's new bicycle. Marilyn was from out of state visiting people just up the concreted alley from our house. Of course she was a very pretty girl with long flowing blond hair and almost as beautiful as the new bicycle she flaunted. Now that was hard to take because I didn't have any bicycle, even an old beat up set of wheels, and I really got lathered wanting to ride that bike.

Finally the day came and Marilyn told me I could ride it whenever I wanted; the deal was that I could come to the house and take it for a spin if she weren't using it. So I did.

Of course, you know that Fate wouldn't miss a chance like that. So Fate nailed me.

I was going down the alley, newly paved concrete that it was, with enough speed to impress any of my pals if they happened to see me. Past the halfway mark the alley flattened out and started a slight upgrade. At that very point a man backed out of his garage directly in front of me and the bike. I tried to stop but the brakes wouldn't hold well on the gravel littering the road and those brakes made the wheels slip as I turned

sideways sliding into the side of the car, running board and all. Goodbye one bike.

Of course I had a badge of honor, a rather deep gash on the left leg below the knee and on the inside of the leg. I point out the scar at the slightest invitation, still being obvious countless years later. It's there if my wife or anyone ever needs to identify my body.

My dad replaced the bike but I don't remember any particular scolding or punishment except my father saying something about it being a stupid thing to do.

To add insult to injury, remember that it was a girl's bike. A boy's bike would never have led me into such a dangerous situation.

It was many years later before I had another bicycle experience. It was 1943 when I was teaching at the highly-touted Kemper Military School. I had been in charge of busloads of about 500 cadets going to a dance at an exclusive young ladies school at nearby Columbia, Stephens college, and had a blind date—my first and only blind date. She was a charming young teacher, Carol Hanson of Minnesota. We clicked and were married in August 1943, setting up residence in an apartment in the home of Dr. and Mrs. Wolf on Riverside Drive. (How's that for a memory pull-up from fifty years ago?)

The problem was that we were too poor to own a car so I bought a bicycle in order to shorten my three mile walk to school. Carol usually walked to town for groceries but spent most of the day in that remote apartment with only a radio and a magazine for entertainment; how boring it must have been for her.

My trip from school took me through the downtown area, past the county jail where my grandfather had reigned as sheriff many years ago, past the garage where a man had been killed as he welded a metal barrel which exploded in his face. It had contained traces of a fuel. The route also passed a modern apartment building where, as a high schooler seven years earlier I had gone to pick up a date; when she opened the door I had my first encounter with a full size adult great Dane dog. That immense animal jumped up, put both paws on my shoulders and I thought was going to bite my head off. No, he only licked my face. I was scared to death because his head was as big as a horse's head.

All right! All right! I'll move along. Back to the bicycle.

I was returning home from school late one fall afternoon, coasting full speed ahead down that long Spring street hill, both hands on the handlebars, wearing a new winter coat, gloves, headgear, enjoying the crisp fall air.

When, to my astonishment, I was holding aloft the completely detached handlebars, riding high and free of the cycle.

They had come loose. Detached.

In a second the front wheel twisted, the bike collapsed and I went down, moving fast, and skidding on my shoulder, shredding the new coat. Luckily I could keep my face away from the pavement.

The shaft of the handlebars had apparently been broken and welded together by the manufacturer, passing it on to the poor retailer, Sears in Kansas city, from whom I had bought it as new. Although I don't remember the minute details, I recall how generous they were to me in replacing everything, including the new coat.

That was my first and only important claim against a retailer but I certainly remember the kindliness of that huge firm. So much so that the very day I write this, many years later, I just purchased two Sears Diehard batteries, one for each of our cars.

Boys of that genre always wanted to do something to make a little money. Jobs were scarce during depression days and if a lad could find one the pay was almost minuscule. So, to meet my needs, I decided to raise guinea pigs. For cages I obtained a couple of orange crates and some chicken wire and

VICTORIA

put them together. From someone I purchased a couple of animals and provided them with adjoining apartments.

There are a couple of things to remember about guinea pigs. First, they create a mess which insults the senses almost beyond human endurance. Second, they are very amorous and think nothing of chewing through one-inch wood to reach their mate, so I was constantly building and repairing cages. It would have helped had I known anything about raising animals and about building cages with wire floors or at least sloping floors. As it was there was a constant stink in the back yard and parents always upset at me and the pigs.

One Smelly Fish

I hope my children ask me about certain events while I'm still alive. Not like me. In writing these bits of memoirs I frequently think—

> "How great it would be if I could ask
> Mother or Dad when this event occurred.
> They were 25 years older and would
> remember."

But, alas, it's too late to do that.

The train with the heavily loaded flatbed car pulled in during the night.

I don't remember whether it was the M.P. (Missouri Pacific) or the Katy (Missouri, Kansas and Texas—"Katy" for K.T.) but it brought the huge load into town and parked it on a siding at the foot of Spring street.

To make this story good I should tell about the awful stench, how we could smell the rotting carcass a block up the hill, how the stench was so strong that Dad said to Mother at six A.M., "Mary, what's that awful smell?"

Of course she didn't know either, at the moment.

But soon we were to learn.

A promoter had obtained the carcass of a large whale and was touring the midwest, maybe the whole country, and, for a fee, one could go look at it. The smell, a block away, required no fee.

Of course everyone went to see it.

A whale!

A real whale!

Even though it was dead, it was indeed a ral whale.

They had it laid out on a long flatbed train car, this enormous mammal.

Yes, it was big. As one old farmer said, "That's the biggest damned thing I ever saw."

I've personally seen hundred pound catfish which hang over both sides of a model T ford, but this monster was as long as the flatbed car. That's as long as a cattle car full of beef going to market.

"Look at that damned big thing," said Tommy Harris, "and smell it. It must be rotten."

"Doesn't matter," said Harold Morris, "I think I'm going to puke."

Anyway, we had paid our twenty-five or fifty cents and that night the train hitched up the genuine Pacific Ocean whale and hauled it to the next town.

The next morning we all breathed easier.

This was some time about 1930.

Uncle John's Batteries

My uncle John (that's the Democrat who married into our Republican family) was another favorite uncle, as was his wife, my aunt Gladys. I had a rare opportunity to visit with them for a night or two and always enjoyed myself, because they were nice people.

John and Gladys Sites lived on a hill out of Blackwater, in the family home which I think had been built by John's father, whom they called "The Captain" for what reason I don't know.

Aunt Gladys always had lovely flowers outside her brick home and a big, cool front porch to sit on. She had chickens and other fowl and was a superb cook. Years later after my dear mother died, it was Aunt Gladys who remembered my fondness for wild persimmon pudding and made it for me.

In fact, elsewhere in this book appears a brief description and recipe of persimmon pudding.

Their house was unique in many ways. First, it was brick and cozy compared to the usual frame houses. Also, it had electricity. While other people were waiting anxiously for electricity to "come down the road," which ultimately happened after the Rural Electrification Act was passed, John had installed a home power factory.

No, it wasn't windmills. It was called the Delco Battery System, a series of large batteries arranged in the basement, which supplied the power to light the house and maybe a little of the outdoors. All I can remember from my boyhood days is those glorious light fixtures inside the house—just like we had in town. My cousin, Tom, their son, remembers that the system was in place when he was a child in the late nineteen-thirties and remained so until 1939 when power lines reached the farm. It was a good way to get the jump on others until the power lines finally came down the road.

It also taught me that as Uncle John, that ingenuous man, once said, "Bill, there's more than one way to skin a cat."

Grandpa Charlie was a Man

Charlie Hull was a man. As a boy I always knew this but how do I describe him? To me he was that big, strong man with the mustache, who always greeted me kindly but in whom I was somewhat in awe. Well, why not? He hanged a man.

That was when he was sheriff, of course. I can still remember that awful jail in Madison and that barn behind the jail wherein the hanging occurred. Was it truly during grandpa's reign as sheriff or was it at some earlier date? As an adult I'm not sure, but as a child, I was scared of those seemingly dark cells where they locked up people and of the sometimes drunks I could hear singing therein.

Grandpa Charlie was indeed the progenitor of all those Good Ol' Boys, those men who probably copied and idolized him in every way possible, one of the original Good Ol' Boys of the country.

I know he was a man of great strength, both physically and in character. He loved fun. He liked people and he like Hill and Hill bourbon. The few people alive who can remember him today speak very well of him. They liked him well enough at the time to elect him to public offices for twelve years.

He had the strong will of the Hulls but don't call it "temper." Once, occording to his son Pat, the two of them were driving in Pat's new car, probably the 1928 Chevy. A man in a bigger car kept pulling alongside them on the country roads, goading them to race, then dropping back. After this had occurred repeatedly, my grandfather became irked and told Pat to make the man pass.

Grandad had Pat pull alongside the culprit. With the two cars abreast, granddad leaned out of his passenger's seat and pointed a 32-caliber pistol at the man's head, saying something like, "You son-of-a-bitch, drop back." Probably scared the man half to death, but he did drop back and they never saw him again.

He was a good shot with that pistol too. Although he owned a powerful forty-five, he preferred the little thirty-two, saying it could do anything necessary. On another occasion, Pat told me of a time when his father shot a jackrabbit in the head as it loped down a country road before the car. That required excellent timing and skill.

By today's standards he lived a gusty life. He married a lovely woman, raised a good family, lived to be an old man in good health and had all the creature comforts he needed, probably the greatest being holiday eggnog made of pure farm cream, fresh eggs and lots of good old southern bourbon.

He was a man but he didn't try to prove it by using rough language. Probably the extent of his cursing was "Damn it, Maw, isn't supper ready yet?"

"Maw" as he and his children called her, had been a beautiful girl as Lillian Ashmead, and she became a lovely elderly lady, a motherly woman with so much long white hair it seemed to reach her knees when she combed it out. She was a dear soul who was kind to us kids. Whatever we wanted, it was ours. Whatever we wanted to do was fine with her. And whenever she hugged us she seemed warm and stifling from the heat of the big woodburning kitchen cook stove.

My children only once saw a woodburning cook stove in full use. Those big old ranges had a firebox on one side where the wood was burned. The rest of it was mainly a big oven and a big flat top, under which the heated air circulated and provided warmth. Hot water was heated in an adjoining section on some of the ranges. Biscuits were baked in the oven almost every morning of my grandmother's life. It was from seeing her make biscuits that I learned to mix pastry with my fingers in preference to using a pastry cutter. But before the biscuits were baked, that big oven door was left open to help warm the kitchen on frosty mornings. Many a pair of cold feet and hands were thrust into the open door of this type of range in the early days of this country.

She worked hard, waited on others, slaved for her family, and then one day when she was an old lady, she broke her hip. The hip was slow to heal, complications developed and the dear old lady died. Grandfather lived on, without enthusiasm, for a few years, as a superb piece of human machinery gradually wearing out. He reminded me of Oliver Wendell Holmes' "Wonderful One-Hoss Shay," the poem of the buggy that was built so superbly that when it finally wore out, everything fell apart simultaneously and it collapsed. It was somewhat that way with him. You could see the aging, the drooping, the loss of strength, until one day there was nothing, just a very old man. When he died, I felt a great loss, which even my own parents didn't realize, for I had loved him for his solidity, his quiet dominance, and his determination. People either liked or disliked this fine old man but they never ignored him.

Named after the beloved Ulysses S. Grant, he was just one of a large family, but he is the one to whom my daughters and granddaughters owe their paternal bloodlines and one of whom they can be proud, as they can of Lillian.

Isn't it great when one can be proud of one's parents and grandparents?

Bell's View Park and Lady Apples

Bell's View park in Madison was really an overlook park, much like the much larger Harley park across town. Both provided spots to overlook the Missouri river far below and to see across the river into Victor county. In years of the many floods they were popular places to see the bottom lands overwhelmed with water.

Colonel C. C. Bell, a prominent man in Madison and in the county, had donated the land for Bell's View Park at High and Eighth streets, diagonally across from the spacious Bell home. Colonel Bell had been a Madison leader and philanthropist. He started as an apple shipper, then developed his own large orchard and specialized in a small apple called a Lady apple, which was very sweet and juicy.

They were extremely popular in eastern markets and in 1937 his was the only known orchard able to ship train carloads of the valuable fruit.

Bell had been an important man in Madison, where he was three-term mayor, vice-president of a major bank, and an early legislative candidate. E. J. Melton says he donated the park to the citizens of Madison and supported the park for many years.*

I'm only personally sure that Bell's View Park was a quiet sunshiny place where one could stand and look over the imaginary parapets, wondering what the river looked like in the days when paddle wheelers steamed up from New Orleans with their loads of furniture and prize lumber for building fancy houses on the river bluffs of Madison; some of those stately homes built by the river barons and other early settlers still exist.

On many occasions when I was a boy and heard stories about Colonel Bell, I wished I could have known him . . . a man who died long before I was born but a man who 1) was the first mayor to pass a law prohibiting stock of all types from the public streets, 2) was present when President McKinley was assassinated, 3) joined a Buffalo Hunt Train from Kansas City, 4) conceived the idea of the International Apple Shippers association, started that group and became its honorary life president, and 5) a member of the committee to notify Benjamin Harrison of his nomination as Republican presidential candidate.

What a man he must have been! Any boy reading and hearing of all those accomplishments would have wanted to know more about him, to emulate him.

All I could do was to look out over the wide Missouri from his park and admire him for his achievements.

---

*"History of Missouri," by E. J. Melton, © 1937.

Without TV, We Sang

Those were the good old singing days. We sang in school, in church, and at home. I will always remember my mother's sweet voice around the house and how she encouraged me and Charles to sing the songs she taught us.

During and after the war to end all wars we sang such great troop morale builders as "Over There" and "My Buddy" which, in spite of the sad elements therein helped us picture the poor cold soldiers huddled down in wet trenches while being gunned by the Big Berthas of Germany. Those of us who learned those songs still know them and use our bathroom baritones to keep them fresh in our memories.

Then, how about the time when someone introduced "My Blue Heaven" which was a sentimental song about a young couple's home and how to reach it, followed by "Lucky Lucky Lindbergh" with that great sub-title "The Eagle of the U.S.A." He was an eagle too, maybe even a god because little boys swooped around with toy airplanes mimicking how that brave young man went clear across the Atlantic in a plane of doubtful ability—and made it.

And somewhere in there came "Just Molly and Me"—no, that's a line from "My Blue Heaven." So, I never told you I was perfect.

If you wish, I could sing you the lines of "The Prisoner's Lament" about the jailbird who wished he had wings and could fly away to his woman.

Pop songs are a wonderful way to remember a decade. In recent years will it be the Beatles' songs, or Elvis's tunes, or more currently, television sitcom theme songs, which will bring back memories for people fifty years from now?

The Cream Separator

I never thought I'd forget the manufacturer's name of that cream separator I sometimes turned at Uncle Seb's farm when I was a boy. I visited him and Aunt Flora, both now gone, God rest their souls, at their place at Lamine, just atop the hill overlooking the Lamine river.

The separator was a tool which separated the cream from the milk, so the valuable cream could be sent to the creamery for butter-making purposes. It was a rather large piece of equipment with bowl on top for the raw milk and funnels coming out for the cream and the residue—the skim milk.

I shared a bit of nostalgia with friends recently at the Kanabec County Historical Society and Museum in Mora, Minnesota, where I saw one of these old machines on display. Both George (last name unknown) and I remembered how one turned these things until they reached a certain pitch. If it weren't being turned fast enough, all the cream wasn't being removed and someone would yell at you to turn faster. Rev it up, it isn't screaming loudly enough.

But there were lots of memories of Aunt Flora and Uncle Seborn. There was the blacksnake in the cottonwood over the lawn swing; Uncle Seb disposed of it by proper application of the twelve-gauge shotgun. Also there was the self-sown watermelon seed which sprouted and grew near the cistern by the back door. With it being so hot and dry, Aunt Flora sustained it by throwing her dishwater on it, so it could live. After many weeks, it came harvest time for that melon and I was fortunate to be there. One bite and—ugh—it tasted of soapy dishwater. So it was destroyed.

Camping in the Orchard

It was always hot. Sweat came to the brow and under the arms easily during the early thirties. Everyone seemed to smell of sweat. Clothes became stale easily. Housewives didn't have electric washing machines as handily as today, and to keep the family's clothing free of dirt and smelling sweet was a backbreaking job.

Tom and I were always working on some merit badge or the other, always thinking ahead toward that day when we'd be Eagles. We knew we would make it sometime, but it took a lot of work.

We decided in the spring to qualify for our overnight by sleeping out in an orchard on the hill of old 40 west of town. It was a hot night and we knew we wouldn't need much except a pup tent and we'd sleep in our underwear. The problem was that we didn't know there was a chance of rain.

Rain! Hell! It never rained anymore. So that night we cooked our small rations over a little fire, using my very small skillet that must have been a World War I relic from Uncle Seb or someone. What a tiny thing it was. Anyway, we ate a bite and then pitched our tent.

Like all good Boy Scouts we knew everything there was about pitching a tent—or so we thought. We pitched it on the slope in the apple orchard with lots of good ol' trees around us. And we knew enough to ditch it all the way around—just a token—because no rain would fall. Suffice it

to say we only dug a little ditch, so small it wouldn't have handled dew. Then we went to bed, talked until exhausted and went to sleep, snug in that darned little pup tent.

In the middle of the night we were awakened by a strong wind, flashing lightning and a downpour. That rain came down like it was going to bring the last four years' average up to date in thirty minutes. And it all came rushing down that slope where we were located. Water was everywhere.

We had water running into the tent from holes in the top; there was water rushing across the bottom where our blankets were strewn and water inundating us. One of us said, "What the devil are we doing here?"

At nearly that precise moment a terrible crash and nearby shock of lightning made us jump nearly out of our underwear. But nothing seemed to have occurred.

Well, we stuck it out but we'll never forget that night. We finally went back to sleep for a while only to awaken stiff and cold, wet to the skin. We had to climb through the branches of a downed apple tree directly across our tent opening. That crash of the night before had been a direct hit within ten feet of us!

You can imagine how our folks felt when we came straggling in early in the morning, a pitiful sight for two future Eagles.

I've often wondered where we borrowed that junky pup tent.

There Goes Uncle Bill

Uncle Bill (William Jasper Hull) was an engineer on the Missouri Pacific railroad lines. He ran the freight trains on the river route from Kansas City to St. Louis, having this senior position for many years. He was my father's uncle, not mine.

The route which Uncle Bill ran went through the village of Lamine, about a half-mile from my grandfather's house in the flats near the Lamine river, a tributary of the Missouri.

In my boyhood days it was common for all the family of my grandfather (Uncle Bill's brother) to gather at the Lamine house. Every birthday saw us together. Thanksgivings and Christmases we assembled to fill the little house to overflowing. Everyone knew Uncle Bill's schedule, which always seemed to coincide with the second round of eggnogs. The train would whistle mournfully for the Lamine highway/railroad crossing but it seemed to us that an extra blast or two was given in salute to my grandfather's fmaily. Everyone else thought so too, because the cry would go up "There Goes Uncle Bill" and we kids were conditioned to rush to the porch to count the long row of cars, wondering if it would reach a hundred, and to wave frantically to Uncle Bill who just had to be the engineer on duty that day.

In later years when my father and mother retired to a small farm near Blackwater, still in Fulton county, that same river route ran through that nearby town and the tracks bent around to go through the bottom land near my parents' house. When the train blew the blast for the Blackwater crossing it seemed again that an extra blast saluted us. To that day, when Uncle Bill was long deceased, some of us in memory would take up the old cry of "There Goes Uncle Bill." Who knows, maybe Uncle Bill still does ride that route on particular days when he wants to help some younger, less experienced engineer get through that long trip.

It always seemed to me that it would have been appropriate at Uncle Bill's funeral service to have someone softly give the old greeting of "There Goes Uncle Bill."

The Man who Built Bonfires under Model T Fords

Uncle Arth (Henry Arthur Hull) was a man to remember and respect. The youngest of nine children of Richard Romulus Hull, he stays fresh in my memory as a lovable man of great interest to a boy.

Scenes I remember all my lifetime are of him sitting under a tree in their yard, cracking and eating butternuts, a rarity which I had never seen before or since. I remember how delicious they were. More than that, on one particular visit to Uncle Arth's and Aunt Bess's he had been building a fire under a model T to get it started. It wasn't really that cold but, for some reason, he had pushed the car out of the garage onto the bare earth driveway and had a small fire warming the crankcase.

Once I watched in fascination as he tried to start that old car. He jacked it up, put it in gear, kicked the hell out of it and it took off. He was a marvel!

He had run a sawmill. He knew all there was to know about catching catfish in the Lamine river, and he was missing three fingers on one hand. As an infant, he had walked close to the woodpile where his brother, my grandfather Charles, a boy himself, was chopping wood. Arthur caught his foot in his baby dress, stumbled, and put his hand down on the chopping block just as the axe came down . . . and lost the three middle fingers of his left hand. Bess emphasized once to me that it was indeed the left hand because some photographer printed a photo in reverse, showing the maimed right hand. All of his life Arth used the little finger and the thumb of that hand with such dexterity that I doubt if he ever thought of himself as being handicapped.

Who would ever forget a two-fingered great uncle who ate butternuts, who built fires under automobiles and who knew everything about catfishing?

Aunt Bess seemed to be the world's best bread baker, except for my mother, of course. Did we always visit them just as the hot bread came from the oven, or was she simply always baking? I recall the odors from her kitchen and the rewarding slice of warm bread with fresh country butter lathered atop it. She was also the most enthusiastic rocker ever, rocking in her chair so vigorously that her feet would leave the floor and then come crashing down for more propulsion. In later years I saw an advertisement of a whiskey called something like "Old Rocking Chair" with an illustration showing a keg strapped under a rocker, where it sloshed and aged. Of course I knew that Aunt Bess would have had no part of that procedure.

They were wonderful people and I'll treasure my memories of them.

Crippled Sis

With all the relatives we had in the county, I suppose my parents simply didn't have time to place each family all on an equal basis, so we didn't see too much of my father's Aunt Lyd and Uncle Lou. I can only remember going to their house a few times as a child and can never remember them coming to ours.

But what a thrill it was to go to that house. As I recall it, there was something about it that was mysterious. It was off the road, across some rolling land, up a barnyard slope to the house. It was either a brick or a dark wood. Apparently I was not too observant of the exterior.

But the inside of that house I remember. To begin with, there was something different about the Hallers. They were "Catholic." I suppose the word "Catholic" had been whispered in my presence and it was something different. I knew "they" lit candles and perhaps "they" were something like the Ku Klux Klan, whom I had once seen burn a cross. And my brother had been taken to the hospital to die—and it was a "Catholic" hospital. So here was an area that, as a child sixty years ago, I didn't know about and probably wasn't too interested in.

But, oh, that house and those lovely people! Aunt Lyd I recall as being a very large woman, as were most of the Hulls, and a wonderful hostess. She treated us well and that house was a warm haven in winter—a house that exuded her glow.

We sat, I believe, in the kitchen, and Uncle Lou would bring out his famous home-made wine. I can remember being permitted to taste the dandelion wine, which was better than I could make in later years.

To get that wine, he would take a lighted coal oil lamp and go through a trap door in the kitchen, down into some *sanctum sanctorum.* That pit was so threatening to a child, I wouldn't accept the invitiation to go too, but I could see the flickering light on the rows of bottles. Of course it was only a cellar with an opening through the floor.

And from that room where we sat, there ran a stairway to the second floor, a very narrow stairway; it seemed to me to be so small that no one could possibly get up it. I never got the chance, but it intrigued me.

In the parlor was the *piece de resistance . . .* a player piano. To understand what this meant to me, you need to know there was very little music in our home other than my mother's singing. Radio was limited to a few crystal sets and there was no piano at home. Here was a piano that gave out wonderful music which I could produce myself. If you want to see real ecstasy sometime, put a seven-year-old child on a player piano stool and let him produce his own music.

I haven't even mentioned their daughter, whose real name was Marie, but I didn't learn that for many years because the extended family called her "Crippled Sis." Sometimes, just "Sis."

As a child I wasn't precocious, but I was indeed sensitive. And the family name for this lovely soul bothered me in a way a child couldn't understand. It was bad enough to be around her, to see her crippled arms and feet, but to call her "Crippled Sis" seemed cruel, even brutal, to me and made me uncomfortable.

She was the daughter of my grandfather Hull's sister, Lydia Hull, and Louis Haller. Thus she was my father's cousin and my second cousin. Apparently she had been born with clubbed hands and feet. When I was eight she was twenty-eight which made her a grown woman. She was large because of her sedentary life; she had a superb smile and a laugh that lit up the entire house. Perhaps the world was so different at the end of the century, when she was born, that it was realistic to call her "crippled" rather than to try to nurture her with love and gentleness. I blamed her parents and the whole family for years for being so callous.

With all of that difficulty, with that inability to move, to feed herself well, to live as a natural person, Marie still lived to be married at age forty and to succumb at age seventy-seven.

She lived with her parents and brothers in the Martinsville area of Fulton county, Missouri, in the house I have described as "the foreboding house on the hill."

It was indeed a fascinating place.

Uncle Walter's Coming Home

My mother flurried around the hot kitchen. The wood cook stove, which dominated the room, had long ago changed from gentle warmth of the cool fall morning, to a monster overheating the room.

"More wood," said Mother, turning to me with a swirl of flour filling the area.

She had run the wild persimmons through the colander and added a pint of water to the original quart of the puckery fruit, but they were no longer puckery because we had gathered them after the frosts had wrinkled them and caused them to drop to the ground.

"Now for the eggs," she said and beat in three big country fresh eggs with salt, a teaspoon of allspice, some cinnamon, and two cups of sugar. Mother always liked things very sweet.

Three cups of flour went into the mixture, another pint of water, plus a whole quart of milk.

"Oh, I don't have any raisins," she lamented, "then we'll just have to leave them out."

And the whole liquid batter went into the moderate oven for an hour.

The wild persimmon is one of Missouri's greatest assets, although everyone may not know it as well as do some of us aficionados. Eating one fresh, ripe and succulent fruit, spitting its six or more seeds at the same time, is one of life's really fine pleasures.

Any Missouri native who doesn't have a personal persimmon tree tucked away somewhere, is at a loss. I can drive to one at the edge of Madison, on "Old 40" as they call the former route of U.S. 40. Also I can walk in two directions on my dad's former farm in Fulton county and find the two outstanding persimmon trees thereon. They are unusual because they bear heavily, not because of their gargantuan size but because when they are not in fruit they are unimposing trees which appear like brush.

There it grows, loaded with the little one and one-quarter inch brown fruit seemingly ignored by everyone who passes. But any true lover of persimmons knows they are best when fallen to the ground. That means they have ripened fully, either having been frosted or frozen before the tree shed them. While still on the tree they can be as bitter as quinine, a taste which has probably caused many people to think they didn't like the fruit.

Persimmon pudding. If ever there were ambrosia, this was it. The wild persimmon was plentiful then in Missouri. today it is a lucky family that can claim its own tree. The pudding is deliciously different.

If it weren't persimmon pudding, then it was either angel food cake or plum puddings, or both. Those puddings, baked in cans and kept waiting for that special guest, were then removed and steamed, served with a sauce.

What was it that set her off onto such a cooking spree? Always a superb cook, something was unusual these days. Then she'd make her announcement.

"Uncle Walter's coming home."

This was said somewhat like the preacher on Sunday morning saying, "The world will surely come to an end tomorrow."

Those were magic words. Her brother Walter, one of the twins, was coming back for a visit, all the way from California.

In the early thirties when Uncle Walter came from California, or my father's uncle came from Seattle, it was an event. Transportation was slow and it was such a trip was like going to Asia might be today.

Walter was obviously a favorite brother, if not the favorite of my mother. He had broken away from the family, moved to California, become a successful railroad executive and a Shriner. He had traveled the hot sands to another land and made his mark. My mother held him up to me to be emulated, which was probably one of the reasons she was so ambitious for me and so proud the day many years later when I became a Shriner.

But to us kids Walter wasn't envisioned as a great man in a fez coming across the country, but as a hardy man racing hellbent for election across the dusty dessert, kicking up rooster tails of sand as he drove wide open for home.

When he came "home" we had one of the few happy Moore gatherings; usually we assembled only for funerals. But Walter's homecoming was joyous. We gathered at Grandmother Moore's for fun and food. Grandmother gave us homemade grape juice in her special glasses with the blue indented grapes on the side. We kids played in the grape arbor and in the new storm cellar, the garden, even the house. And how great it was to be in the house when it didn't smell of pinks and carnations because of the deceased in the other room in a casket.

If I were lucky, Dad would even take me next door to visit Uncle Jim Steger's woodworking shop behind his house. There were lathes, drills, saws, all of those foot-powered tools I didn't know existed in a room full of spicy wood shavings. I wanted to live in that room forever.

At the end of the day we'd all pile into our cars and go home; within a few more days Uncle Walter, after visiting at our various homes, would return to California—wherever that was.

The Printer's Devil

When I was twelve I first met Elston J. Melton, known to about everyone as "E.J.," the editor of the local weekly newspaper. Although the name seemed to change occasionally, I remember it as "The Fulton County Missourian," of Madison, Missouri.

Elston was a father figure for me in many ways and I was his printer's devil. If you don't know what a printer's devil is, consider it sort of an apprentice to a printer. That "devil" was supposed to do anything the printer wanted done, and to jump to it quickly. But Mr. Melton was not a demanding boss.

I became a printer's devil at age twelve which practically put me into the category of kids working in sweat shops in New York City.

Mr. Melton would sit at his Linotype machine writing his stories for the forthcoming issue. That machine was a tall device filled with used metal slugs (lines of type which had been previously used) and melted down within the machine. As the operator sat at the keyboard and typed his story, forms called "keys" would drop down into the machine and form the base for a line of type, whatever the width of that would be for that particular newspaper. It was hot work and Mr. Melton, who really ran a one man shop, would sit by the hour writing his stories and composing long galleys of the lead lines of type formed by the machine.

Then they were moved to a flat stone, which really was a stone in this case, and fitted into a framework from which a whole page was printed.

If interested, call around your city and ask if there is still any place you can go to see an old-fashioned Linotype machine still being used. They are probably all museum pieces by this time.

While I was writing stories, or working on the paid subscriber list, Mr. Melton would be turning out stories of crime and punishment as fast as possible on that infernal machine.

I well remember the first crisis that occurred during my employment.

Mr. Melton was working on the stone, making up pages for the next issue. He took a framework the size of the page, and filled it in with columns of this set metal type, probably six columns, which were tightly fit together so they would not drift when the printing occurred, and were tightened into position by expandable keys around the perimeter. This meant that whole page of type was within that one framework, which was so tightly put together that it could be lifted and carried to the flatbed press, laid alongside another such page, and the press would print the two pages simultaneously. However, it was a very heavy form and the danger of spilling it was horrendous; to spill it would mean sorting out all of those lines of type and fitting them back into the framework.

E.J. said to me, when he had finished locking up the form, "Bill, you want to put this on the press?" Meaning do you want to pick up this solid form of type and carry it across the room to place it on the flatbed press.

"Sure," I said, cocky as only an ignoramus could be.

I walked to the "stone" work table, pulled the form slightly toward me, lifted it a fourth of an inch as I had seen him do many times, to be sure each line was securely locked in place, and started to pick it up.

Mother of God! That thing was so heavy I couldn't budge it, much less pick it up and carry it. I turned to the boss.

"Mr. Melton, I can't handle it. If that's part of my job you might as well let me go now, because it's too heavy for me." He laughed and said, "I know that, Bill. I guess I was just testing." Testing! No kid of my age and angular build could have handled that thing. I bet it weighed at least a zillion pounds.

We became good friends. He appreciated my interest and encouraged me. He paid me a little more each year until I was nearing high school graduation age.

By that time he had sold the newspaper or perhaps succumbed to the more successful *Daily News* and he had started to write his history of the county. He was a good one to write it because he knew everyone in the county and probably had many secrets up his sleeve. During this time he needed an assistant (probably considered more like a secretary) and I was it. I typed forever on that old Underwood Number Five until either it or I wore out. I learned how to apply thin oil to an exhausted typewriter ribbon to rejuvenate it, leaving it soak for a day or two and substituting a previously oiled one in the interim. Mr. Melton knew a lot of tricks of the trade, yet he produced a fine book, a copy of which I still keep in an important spot because E.J. Melton started me on my path as a writer.

The Teach Aleen

Mid-state Missourians will immediately challenge the spelling of the "Teach Aleen," but wait and they will realize I'm using a common mispronunciation for the Petite Saline, a mid-state creek or river of various reputations.

At least I never heard anyone pronounce the name as the original French explorers named it. Obviously the title refers both to the size and the saltiness of the water.

But it did have fish at one time, nice carp of taking size.

We had a picnic somewhere on the banks of the Petite Saline when I was in my early teens. At that same age I had my first pistol, a 22 caliber semi-automatic. Now the danger of a kid having both a pistol and shells is that he will fire it or explode.

I didn't want to explode. But there was that creek with carp so big I could have knocked them over the head with a pole. But, I thought, why not just shoot one or two? I'd have fun and get some nice fish in the funning.

Nobody told me it wouldn't work. Neither Dad nor others present said, "Bill, you can't shoot fish in a barrel." So I tried.

Bang! went the pistol, aimed precisely at a big carp practically on the surface of the water. The fish just swam away gently.

BANG! BANG! BANG! I kept trying and kept failing. Remember that I had a drawer full of National Rifle Association

badges; I had some skill at hitting a target, none of which helped me then.

Finally I could see what was happening.

The bullet would hit the water directly above the fish and change the angle so it passed directly by the object. The water was deflecting the bullet and saving the fish.

No matter how many times I went bang, bang, no matter how many times I tried to change the spot of aim, the trajectory always saved the fish, and I felt stupid.

I'd liked to have returned to the family on the bank with a tree switch full of six- or seven-pound carp, but you know what happened.

Nobody helped. But everybody knew. The only comment was "Why do you waste all your cartridges? They cost money."

Uncle Neil and the Alky

In 1928 my father, Aubrey Grant Hull, had an auto collision with a culvert out in Kansas. I can well remember the telling of the event. How he somehow managed to extricate himself from the wreckage and walk to a farmhouse a mile or two away. How he knocked on the door after dark and almost caused a housewife to have a heart attack. He was so badly cut facially that folds of his skin fell over his eyes, and away from his jaws, while blood was everywhere. Anyway, he survived with no permanent problems—but this part of the story now concerns Uncle Neil.

Cornelius was not a teetotaler but he certainly was an abstainer. I don't know whether he had previously bouted with booze or just didn't like it, but I had rarely seen him take a drink.

When the news of my dad's wreck reached Madison I was ten and we were living across the street from the grade school. Mother wanted to go to Dad at once but I was considered too young and was left behind. So Uncle Pat drove in his new 1929 automobile, which he had just obtained. Along with him that cold December went Mother, Uncle Neil, and my grandfather, Charles Grant Hull.

Pat (Clarence Edward) and my grandfather were in the front seat and my mother and Neil in the back seat. It was a long trip in those days from mid-Missouri to mid-Kansas on roads that were quite primitive. It was a tiring trip and my grandfather took along a bottle, probably of his favorite Hill and Hill bourbon. He offered Pat a drink surreptitiously; they may have had a couple to ease the fatigue and to switch drivers. In the rear seat Neil sniffed and said, "Pat, you'd better stop before you ruin the car." Pat replied, "Why? What's wrong?" Neil then explained that he could smell the "alky" boiling over.

Alcohol was used in radiators in those days because it was so much cheaper than the new anti-freeze, even though it boiled over easily. Pat demurred that everything was all right but, upon Neil's insistence, they stopped and inspected the car.

Of course they made it to Kansas with no problems, eventually bringing my hospitalized father home with his many-scarred face, which gradually healed. The scars disappeared with the years, becoming character lines as he aged into a handsome man with a shock of pure white hair.

As for uncle Neil. He knew better because he smelled alky all the way to Kansas and back and always thought Pat had a remarkable car to let it boil over that often without ruining the radiator.

VICTORIA

Martha, That Beautiful Girl

Martha was a beautiful girl, tall, dark-haired, flashing eyes, graceful, all the things that drew me to her at about eighteen. There was only one problem.

She was Catholic.

The problem was that I didn't know that was a problem. In fact, I didn't know anything about Catholics. What were they? Were they different from us? Was it an important difference?

In the rural America of the mid-south of the thirties, there were different class distinctions. "We" were what sociologists call WASPS (white, Anglo-Saxon Protestants)—ah, but there was a side group of Catholics. I never remember anyone saying a word, or a sneer about Catholics or Catholicism. We were too isolated.

In our poor little town I later learned there were other people. They were the negroes, the Catholics, and a few Italians. Nobody ever mentioned their existence. Both the Catholics and the blacks (thank God we didn't call them "niggers") had their own schools and kept away from us as if they, or us, had the Black Death.

So help me, God, I did not know there were separate schools; I didn't know—was it St. Peter and St. Paul? Was it a Catholic school? What an alienated, unfairly separatist kid I was. Today I hang my head with shame. Now I know I wasn't just the fair-haired boy who won citizenship honors in high school, as the most this or the most that. . . . I was the fair-haired boy among the non-Catholics or the non-blacks.

All of this is an attempt to seek understanding and perhaps sympathy, because I was greatly attracted to Martha, whom I saw repeatedly in her parents' downtown store.

So I asked Martha for a date. She accepted and we had a great time. Her friends and my friends must have had some raised eyebrows, but we genuinely liked each other. We had good clean innocent fun on dates. We were young innocent children.

But it soon appeared that we were not ignored. There were people in the town who noticed and who probably said, "What's that stupid Baptist boy doing, dating our Martha?" or "Why's that pretty Martha going with that Hull boy?"

Those conversations must have been going on. Perhaps Martha's family heard it, perhaps my family, but I never heard it.

Never, that is, until two of the biggest Catholic boys I ever saw came up to me one night when I was alone.

"What are you doing, dating Martha?" they asked, clenched fists at their sides.

"Nothing," I weaseled. "We're just good friends."

"Then quit it, Bill. She's not for you. Don't you know she's Catholic?"

So I was told to keep my place, or else.

Later, I thought I knew how blacks must have felt when they overstepped a line—a foolish imaginary line that only exists in some poor prejudiced people's imagination.

Soon we were going our separate ways anyhow, off to different colleges, and we broke it off. Many years later Martha and I, along with my wife, Carol, had lunch in a different part of the country. I knew then my judgment of character and charm had been right on, but we had been out of synch with our time.

The Cabinet Makers

We called them Uncle Roy and Uncle Jim but their relationship to us was unique. Uncle Roy (1900–1985) was truly my uncle, being my father's brother. Uncle Jim (approximately 1862–1950, which were his spouse's birth/death dates.) He was of another generation than Roy, and was my father's uncle, my great-uncle. His name was Jim Steger, pronounced "Stigger."

These men were both master craftsmen and I don't even know if they knew each other. I only knew Uncle Jim when he was an old man, but boy-oh-boy how I liked to visit him and Aunt Zet, who was my grandfather Hull's sister; they lived next door to my Grandmother Moore in Pilot Grove. Jim had a workshop unlike any I had ever seen before. He had lathes, power drills, power saws and many, many hand tools. Many times I've visualized that antique woodworking shop reestablished as a museum place of craftsman's tools.

Jim's workshop always appeared to have been used immediately before we arrived. The smell of newly cut lumber was so heavy it was like an incense. He used a lot of cedar, which was plentiful in Missouri, and shavings and sawdust mixed with small leftover lumber bits on the floor to the point where one scuffed in it. He burned the bits in a small stove for warmth.

This was prior to electricity so the shop was hand or foot powered. There was a central shaft running across the room,

tied up in some way with footpower he supplied. It was something to see this old gentleman pumping away at something that looked like the remains of a sewing machine, while the energy was transferred to a selected machine across the room.

Among other things, he made cabinets to order. He had made them for his own wife, Zettie, and then by commission for other people. In Pilot Grove there are probably still some of his beautiful pieces, gracing older homes. My dad once showed me how the cabinet doors fit so perfectly, how the hinges closed the doors so they were snug. This was before some of the self-adjusting hinges became available.

He was so skilled he could have been assigned to create and install cabinets in any mansion in the country.

Uncle Roy (Henry Leroy Hull) was, as I said, of another generation. I often heard him called a "card" which meant he was an individual and didn't fit the typical mold. He had a great sense of humor and was always pleasant to me. He and Aunt Ruth and their girls lived in several houses in the county; this probably was during the drought and depression days of the thirties when money and jobs were scarce. It seemed to me that at every house they rented Uncle Roy would make new cabinets for the kitchen; if he didn't make them, he completely remodeled them—and *painted* them. Somewhere I remember lovely white cabinets trimmed in blue striping.

They left their marks, did Uncles Roy and Jim, on their own children and many others like me, who felt their influence and remember their kindnesses. What else is there in life?

Manhood Years

Keeping Cool in
Very Hot Weather

It was hot, so very hot that people who never lived through it have a tendency to question the severity when others speak of it.

In rural Missouri and in cities like St. Louis, that 1936 summer set all time high records. Thirty successive days of temps exceeding the 100 mark were typical of that summer. Terrible results occurred. Cattle died from being overheated, people had heatstroke, some perishing. Crops dried up and blew away, if they even sprouted to begin with. This country wilted under a combination drought and depression that left people literally gasping for relief.

Such a simple thing as getting a night's sleep was a huge problem, a challenge often impossible. A house that was exposed to one hundred or greater heat for hours of the day just didn't cool off at night. People turned garden hoses on their homes in the evening and then went to bed to sweat, kicked off the flimsy sheet which was just as unbearable as a cotton blanket would have been. There was no air moving, rarely a glorious cross ventilation in a stifling house. The only relief possible was to sleep under an electric fan or soaking a bedsheet in water and hanging it up in the room. While it added humidity it also provided a slight cooling. Many people slept outside on a sheet on the grass.

Air conditioning? Hah! Just not available. I don't think even the very wealthy had that luxury. The nearest thing to a cool place was when someone in the Mercantile store put a big fan behind a hundred-pound cake of ice. People flocked into that store, believe me.

The ill were particularly vulnerable because there wasn't much to be done for them. In hospitals, in churches, in homes, people tried to keep out the heat. About all they could do was to close up the house during the day. Mother constantly said, "Close the windows. Pull down the shades. Don't let that sun inside."

Funeral services and regular church services were horrors of discomfort. People usually "dressed up" a little better for these events, and then sweat through their best clothes.

Genuine palmetto fans from Florida were soon replaced by paper fans provided by the mortuaries. These fans drifted away from the mortuaries and people used them at any event.

Kids swarmed to pools, creeks and rivers, just to get wet and hoping to cool off.

As John Morgan said, "My Gawd. It's hot as hell is going to be."

It was.

Those Lovely White-Haired Old Ladies

There's nothing like a grandmother or any other sweet old lady who looks like a grandmother. To me there was Grandmother Hull, Grandmother Moore and Aunt Zet, all in that category.

Grandmothers "in olden days" looked the part. They had accepted their white-haired roles in life, probably because they had neither the money nor the cosmetics to change their positions, or because they faced growing old and white-haired as being normal. It has never been a shameful role and I suspect there was pride in reaching the white-haired stage when so many of their generation had died long ago.

I always think of the preacher who talked at length about living with others in peace, but who said that there probably wasn't a person in his congregation that morning who didn't have an enemy. He asked if any such person were present. One very ancient man arose. After praising the man, the preacher asked him publicly why this had happened. The oldster replied: "Because I outlived all the sons-of-bitches."

Grandmother Hull, whom I saw more frequently than Grandmother Moore, had long white hair. Many times I saw it cascading well below her shoulders as she brushed it thoroughly before gathering it to put it up. It had a richness and a sheen that modern persons would envy and she attained it without the cosmetic aids of today. Grandmother Moore's

VICTORIA

hair was just as white, as that of her neighbor, my Aunt Zet, who actually was my father's aunt, my great aunt.

These ladies were indeed matriarchs, ladies to be obeyed but also nice ladies offering love and kindness, sometimes a refuge.

Maybe love is more kindness than youth realizes. What could be a better definition of love than the memories I have of Grandmother Moore giving me that second half-glass of her homemade grape juice? It came from the arbor alongside the house and was always served from her icebox in special goblets with purple grapes indented as if they were fingerprints. Would a grandmother today trust her valuable crystal to a bunch of kids that had come in from romping outside? Believe me, that was love. I hope that some grandchild has those glasses today and knows their history.

Grandmother Hull also loved us—as we loved her. At her house there were always crowds of people present, yet she always had a warm hug and a kiss for us. How sad when we grew up and hung back slightly.

It was easier for us to understand that Grandmother was Mama's mama because her white hair made it plausible. It must be more difficult for today's children to understand the roles when Grandmother looks just slightly older than Mother.

The First Car

She released the clutch and the car jerked and jumped around the parking lot.

"Push the clutch down," I cried.

She did.

Ingrid, a granddaughter, had just bought her first car, with a little help from grandparents, and was learning to drive the stick shift in a huge, empty parking lot.

A beautiful Honda Accord, seven years old and a direct ancestor of my new model.

Even the color was the same. But the prominent differences were the sixty thousand more miles on her car and it being a stick shift.

I reminisced about my first car.

"It was a 1929 Dodge four-door which I bought in 1936 for college transportation, just like you are doing. It was boxy in design, had upright bench seats, and handled well. I was proud of it and proud that I had the fifty dollars to buy it.

"I remember my first double date in that car. The four of us had gone to a show (movie to moderns), then to Pete's for a coke or a malt, then for a ride up and down Main street to honk at the other kids. The Dodge needed gas so I pulled into a Shell station, told my friend, Jim, who worked the pumps to put in a couple of dollars' worth, at 25 cents a gallon, while the four of us all exploded from the car heading for the rest rooms.

"Yes, Ingrid, I hope your $3,000 used car is half as good as was my $50 car.

"The only problem I ever had was with the starter. It just wouldn't work at times until I would open the hood, remove a plate from the starter case and rotate the insides with a screwdriver. Then—replace the plate, the hold, and give it a try. It would start perfectly. It was a good old car. Yes, old, but it served me well for several years.

"Cars were simpler then. I hope yours does as well.

"Sometimes," I continued, "I think what a shame it is that great Dodge was the only Chrysler product I ever owned. Probably a mistake on my part."

Victoria

Geneva's Great Biscuits

I have a wonderful aunt whom I called "Neenie" as a wee boy because it was the nearest I could come to "Geneva," her true name. She was old—so very old—five years my senior. At the time, as some people say, it didn't seem unusual to me to have an aunt only five years my senior. That was partly true because I never called her "Aunt"—just "Neenie."

We sort of grew up together although she must have shunned me at times. After all, what thirteen-year-old-girl would want to be seen with an eight-year-old boy?

Geneva was the apple of the family eye. Her older brothers, like my father, and her sister, seemed to worship her as an infant, I am told. She was the last of the brood and a child of a couple well along in years.

She lived on the farm most of her life, married, raised a family and has had a good life. Among other things she is the one I remember who cooked and canned meat. Yes, she had jars of cooked sausage, cooked pork and probably beef and fowl. Believe me, when prepared properly, it was delicious.

She also made, and still makes, the best biscuits or rolls anyone in the world ever made. I knew they were something out of this world, being so light and flaky, that I persuaded her to pass on her recipe, which is here for your pleasure.

But she calls them "Butter Crunch Flake-Aparts" not "Biscuits" or "Rolls."

She says to "Dissolve two packages of yeast in one-fourth

cup of warm water. Combine one and one-fourth cups of buttermilk, scalded in a double boiler, with one-third cup of sugar, one-half cup of soft butter (which is also one-fourth of a pound), and two teaspoons of salt. Cool to lukewarm and then add the yeast. Sift together four and one-half cups of sifted flour, one-half teaspoon of soda and add to the above, mixing well. Place in a greased bowl, cover and let raise until double in bulk.

"Then roll out on a floured board to one-fourth inch thickness. Cut into strips two inches wide. Brush with melted butter. Stack five strips together and cut into one inch pieces. Place each stack in greased muffin pans, cut side down. Let rise until double in size, about thirty minutes. Then bake at 400 degrees for fifteen-twenty minutes. Makes two dozen. Then serve and let people pull them apart."

Particularly good if served with good ol' country sorghum syrup.

Total contents equals 2,942 calories and 5,390 mg sodium. If it makes two dozen, each would contain 123 calories and 224 mg of sodium—and a lot of love.

Yes, Geneva Hull Kramer of Blackwater, Missouri, you should receive national acclaim for these Flake-Aparts.

The Mule Shears

There it lay in the debris. It looked like a pair of tinsnips or even weed clippers for a suburban gardener. A single molded piece of spring steel like an oversized pair of scissors.

"They're mule shears," said my dad. "I remember using them many times as a young fellow."

We had picked them up in the yard around the remains of my grandfather Hull's home on the banks of the Lamine river, across the river from Uncle Seb's sawmill and house and Great Uncle Arth's home. The house had been destroyed and the scene was almost obliterated.

I still have the mule shears. Rusted as they are after their initial use maybe eighty years ago, they are the epitome of the past when mules were the source of most farm power.

This little house was the wellspring of the Hulls for me and my generation. There had been bigger and earlier homes but this is the one I remember. From its living room I have the old hall tree with its huge mirror, hooks and bench seat into which we put our overshoes.

From its back porch or "wash room" as it was called, I have the wash table which is a real antique. It is an old card table from a pre-prohibition saloon. At each corner, below the top, is a shelf into which the player's drink could be placed. It is built around an iron framework supporting the shelves, and was patented in 1881.

This is the house where family gatherings were held dur-

ing my boyhood. The Christmas tree with real live candles, the pecan trees in the yard, the third porch which no one ever used, the cistern pump around which we sat and cracked pecans on the concrete, the new well by the barn with water so high in iron it was rusty in color.

Those memories were with me that day, just because we found the mule shears.

The mule shears are in our home today and sometimes visitors look at them and wonder why we keep an old pair of grass trimmers. Little do they know their true history.

To us they are not just mule shears. They are country ham, the smoke house, gumbo bottom land, the old bridge over the Lamine river, the Monkey Ward catalog in the outhouse, Hill & Hill bourbon, and a million other things.

victoria

Down by the River

We followed the old road until it exhausted the sandy area and there were two tracks with the center hump just high enough to rub occasionally against the oilpan of the car as the road now dropped away to the water in front of us.

We stopped at the top of the grade and looked. "It must be a fisherman's camp," Dad said aloud. Here six feet below us was a small encampment which looked as if it were on a beautiful lake.

Then I heard my Dad say it was the Missouri river.

We were not far from Rocheport, wandering Missouri's waterfront towns, always looking for the new and undiscovered mini-Vicksburg or something similar.

We descended the rough area to the water's edge and saw this collection of four little activity centers.

Right in front of us was a machine that had been built with the worker's seat made from the metal seat of an old harrow, or a rake. It was a strange little machine, old and rusty. Very old. Over to the left of it and at the base of a treadle much like mother's Singer sewing machine. Alongside it was a pile of old Prince Albert and Velvet pipe tobacco cans. They had been there so long they were very rusted. I knew this machine engraved messages on the front of old tobacco cans because I had seen them at the state fair in Sedalia last year.

They put the tobacco can into the machine and changed the level to the proper spot for engraving on this particular can. Then the operator moved another lever so it punched the letters on the can. I found one cast aside which said "Johnny Johnson, 1911." Barely holding together, it was badly rusted. It probably had been cast aside for some reason. I wondered how many years this machine had set there and yet I could see fresh newly drawn metallic edges on the blades as if someone had very recently filed the cutting edges. What a weird situation.

Was this a current fishing camp or was it the place the man who lived in the house atop the nearby hill came to get away? Was it an escape spot? I had to know more.

We wandered around the little encampment. Eventually I was drawn into the little shack which had to be the house. My Dad was already inside seated in an old homemade chair, constructed of fairly large well-planed hickory boards supported by rather sturdy tree branches. It created a handsome rocker. "It's comfortable," said my Dad, very much enjoying himself rocking back and forth. I admired that chair.

To his left, by the window, was a large table made a long time ago from what Dad called yellow pine. All four corners were so worn they had become rounded, no longer capable of catching a person in the groin as he walked by. The wood had been highly polished as if a thousand fish had been dressed on it, the oil remaining thereon as a preservative. Although very crude, it was a thing of beauty.

Nearby was a small cast iron stove in which kindling or even heavier wood could be burned on a cold night. This was a serious escape spot where the owner obviously spent entire nights, dressing a duck or a fish or just watching the sun go down over the Missouri and enjoying the serenity of a pipe.

As I looked through the window I saw an elderly lady, estimated age over eighty-five, and very fragile. She wore a puffed-sleeved blouse and a dark skirt so long it reached to the ground. She was sitting in the seat of the machine, perhaps twenty-five feet from us.

"Are you cold?" I called through the door because it was frosty and chilly. She replied, "No, I'm fine. I'm waiting for Jim to return."

Then I realized she had come from the house on the hill and at any moment expected the thump of oars as her husband's skiff pulled ashore. Did she know better? Or should I have known better, because all of this was so ethereal?

When we had first arrived, Marie, Mother's elderly friend, had scrabbled down the six-foot rise to the camp level, as did the rest of us, and repeatedly broke into passionate tears. Nonplused as my folks were, they tried loving her and helping her through the memory rush that caused her to be so upset. We still didn't know the cause, perhaps some very close memory. She had immediately walked over to the Chic Sale. Yes, we were surprised that the man had bothered to build one, here on the Big Muddy. She opened the door, peered inside, reminiscing of her childhood.

Everywhere I expected to open a door or peek in a corner and see a snake. It looked like an ideal spot for reptiles. I couldn't imagine this place existing without at least one copperhead—but I never saw one. Having been a Missourian all my life, I knew about snakes and hated them passionately.

Behind the main house on the beach, if it could be called a house, was a workroom, where it was obvious the man had made etchings. An artist? Impossible.

Here was a large plate, engraved with a handsome scene of the water, with the ducks coming in. It reminded me of the work of the great wildfowl artist whom I was studying at school. How did this unknown early artist print his works? Then I found the material under the table: a collection of very thin pieces of wood, sheets as thin as the thinnest unit of plywood ever made. I pulled one sheet from the center of the pile beneath the bench; it was still white, hidden from exposure to light all those years.

I placed the thin sheet of wood on the stone, much like

the stone in a printer's shop. I found a roller, which was still intact, and then a container of ink, which in all reality would no longer exist. But I rolled the ink onto the etching, turned it upside down over the thinly sliced wood, trying to press it down to create the picture.

Of course it didn't work. The ink was too old and the wood was not properly dampened, too brittle. The pressure was too weak. It was just a pipe dream on my part to bring this back to life.

My father was moving around and getting antsy; Mother was saying, "How much longer are we going to stay here?" But, first, I had to sit in the old man's chair, where Dad had sat for a while. I picked up one of his old pipes and sat there for a few seconds, looking at the sun going down in the river, and wondering what had happened. Had the old man gone down in the river or had he just left this little encampment for the benefit of amateur archaeologists like us?

I sure hated to leave that chair behind.

As we trudged back to the car, my dad said, "I sort of envy him for what he had here. He must have been a Good Ol' Boy.

The Chances a Hitch-Hiker Takes

I was a college freshman, fresh and naive, attending Central Methodist college in Fayette, Missouri, in 1936, commuting from my home about twenty-five miles away.

The Great Depression was still on and I had no transportation, commuting daily in the extended cab of a private-route mail delivery truck running between the two towns. To Fayette in the morning and home in the late afternoon.

This meant I faced problems if I attended evening activities at Central, casually solved by hitching back home late at night, when the traffic was very light and the highway lonely and desolate.

One night, hitching home, after a date, a club meeting, or a basketball game, I stood at the edge of town, in the dark, wondering if a car would ever come along. If so, would the driver take a chance on a tall skinny kid with an outstretched thumb?

Finally one came. And it stopped.

I opened the door and a loud voice said—

"Where you going, kid?"

"Home, to Madison," I replied.

"Okay, then get in. Let's go."

We were driving the winding road, talking the usual unimportant get-acquainted drivel, as my eyes grew accustomed to the dark interior of the Chevrolet. After all, it was pitch black outside.

I thought he was sitting strangely, with his weight over on one hip. Was he crippled? A big man—no, a huge man. It could be anything.

Then I noticed an empty pistol holster on the seat between us.

Good Lord! He has a gun!

And he's sitting on it!

Then my imagination started to run wild.

Was he one of those kooks who assaults men? Or was he planning to rob a poor student, maybe to kill me. But why?

I was wishing I weren't even in that car. Home safely in bed sounded better.

I rested my right hand on the door latch.

By this time he apparently had sized me up as being what he first expected—just another boy too poor to live in the dormitory. And he was reassured.

With a quick motion he reached under his hip and drew out the gun, pointing it at me.

I had the door open and was half out of the speeding car, when he said the words that stopped me.

"Here. Put this in that holster, please, kid."

I closed the door and gingerly slid the Smith & Wesson 38 into the empty holster on the seat between us.

"What the hell!" he roared. "Were you afraid I was going to shoot you?"

"I don't know," I rattled. "How was I to know?"

Then he told me he was a traveling salesman and his company constantly warned their men not to pick up hitch-hikers.

We had a good trip the rest of the way home. He even went out of his way to drive me to my parents' home.

I call that event "The night I almost wet my pants."

Old Mister Hull

Next door to us on main street lived the Thomas family, a nice elderly couple whom even my parents called old. They were, indeed, nearly a generation older than mother and dad.

We kids called the elderly gentleman "Old Mr. Thomas." Why? Just because of our basic virginal cruelty. We had no compassion, only passion, passion to win the roller skate hockey game, played with a tin can for a puck, but not sympathy; no understanding of the elderly.

How little we knew.

Today there are very few children in my suburban neighborhood. A ten-year-old boy across the street and a couple of eight-year-old girls a few houses away.

Do they call me "Old Mr. Hull?" Probably. I'd rather just be considered a Good Ol' Boy.

When they see me walk across the lawn with my hesitating steps they could rightfully call me by that name. My deteriorating lower back causes me to walk stiff-kneed and insecurely, a temporary situation, I pray. It also appears I've dipped too deeply into the brandy bottle.

Not true, neighbors! I'm not drunk. It just hurts so damned much to move in any direction, to stoop to move a sprinkler. It's all so awkward. It makes me remember when I could jump the hurdles at a track meet.

Is it possible? Could I be Old Mister Hull?

No Way!

That was my father when he was age 93.

The Axe-Handle Incident

When the office telephone and other obligations leave me wearied at the end of the day, I take my motorcycle to the country roads, cruising hills, wrapping it around narrow blacktopped roads, using any degree of physical exertion I want. It's exhilarating and also a tremendous release; it can be easy, effortless cruising, or it can be rough riding which demands a lot of physical energy. But I've reduced the latter with a big new bike.

If one likes nature, there are surprises galore in biking. In the wilds of Minnesota, near Canada, on a trail bike, I have toured abandoned logging roads and driven alongside partridge which showed no fear of me. A mile from my suburban Minneapolis home I once drove within fifteen feet of a beautiful fox, who stood still, watching me with no fear. In another direction, a mile from home, near a huge shopping center, I can creep quietly down a gravel road with trees and shrubbery so overgrown one would think one were fifty miles into the bush.

But, to the axe-handle incident.

My old axe is the same axe I've had for thirty years. In spite of two new handles and one new head, it's the same axe. In removing a large shrub, the much-abused handle broke. When I was in Missouri on vacation a few years ago, I remembered I needed a new handle before tackling waiting jobs back home in Minnesota. What better place to buy that

victoria

handle than in the country, where axes are used on every farm. Since I ride the cycle at every opportunity possible, and I was touring the rural hills near my folks' farm, I decided this was the time to buy the axe-handle.

Now it's sad but many people have stereotyped ideas about motorcyclists, particularly when they wear black leather jackets. This situation isn't helped if the rider displays a potential weapon.

Bearing this in mind, you can imagine the reception a cyclist might receive when he rides into a very small country town, wearing a black leather jacket and wanting to buy an axe-handle. Particularly if that small town had recently been vandalized by motorcyclists tipping over tombstones one night.

But I'm ahead of my story.

I don't fit the usual image of the biker, as neither do thousands of other people. I was more typically a middle-aged businessman whose years were obvious in his waistline. And I wore a black leather jacket, not as a sign of belligerence, but under the knowledge that should a rider skid and slide across pavement, the jacket would protect his skin which otherwise, even if wearing synthetics, would be destroyed.

I went into this little town in Fulton county, not the town near which my parents lived, and went to the general store. I didn't slip into town but neither did I roar in. The gentlemen in front of the store couldn't help noticing the bike and the man in the jacket. Greetings were rather aloof. Maybe they saw the chain I carry wrapped around the luggage carrier, to be available when the bike needs locking to a post. Maybe they were just reserved. But they looked me over and followed me into the store.

The proprietor looked rather surprised and my cheery "Good Morning" brought only a laconic grunt. We chatted briefly about where the road led so I wouldn't be too confused as to my directions and then I asked for the axe-handle.

I suppose he visualized me trying to beat him over the head with the handle, smashing store windows and being a true rowdy. And there I was, so naive that it didn't even occur to me that he might be fearful of me. Writing sales letters and other computer work doesn't make one too conversant with that sort of situation. . . . Anyway, he sold me the axe-handle, which I attached to the luggage rack and went out of town, the offending item pointing backwards like some insulting symbol. As I left town I could swear lace curtains fluttered at windows and elderly ladies sighed in relief. Me a threat? Hey, folks, I'm a pussycat.

Later I heard that they'd had problems in that little town . . . problems with cyclists. That group that had raced through the cemetery one night, destroying gravestones had really stirred their anger until it was rumored that those people were quite possibly some of their local farm boys, many of whom owned bikes.

Biking should be fun and more business people should ride them. It's best to bike out of traffic and much less dangerous than being in city traffic. I well remember my provincial New York City friends exclaiming with horror over me riding a cycle. Also I remember a friend who at that time was a senior vice president of either the eleventh or twelfth largest bank in the nation who was defending criticism of "those kids on motorcycles" by saying, "I don't know. I have a businessman friend, my age, who rides a bike. He now has his second, or third one, goes hill climbing, rides in the country, takes his bike with him on trips, has a whale of a time." I was told that the tone in that board meeting changed radically.

So don't put it down. Biking, that is. And don't put the bike down hard on the side either. That can hurt.

But buy your axe-handle when you're driving a car.

Diary of a Septuagenarian

There's only three kinds of pies worth eating.

And they're all fruit pies. Blackberry, apple and gooseberry head the list.

Oh, yes, and wild persimmon should be included because, after the fruits are ripe and have fallen to the ground, they can be made into a great pie, which those who know call a pudding.

Now you can take your cream pies with fluffed up egg whites three inches tall. These are not truly pies in mid-America. Of course they are tasty—the lemon meringue, the meringue-meringue and all those high calorie substitutes for real pies.

My neighbor, old John Hansen, said the other day, "If it ain't an apple or a berry pie, it just ain't a pie."

I agree.

Sure, chocolate pudding pie, black bottom pie in Texas, rhubarb and apple in the midwest, Key lime in Florida, are all soul satisfying masterpieces, but for a hungry man it takes a piece of apple pie to qualify.

Ask the driver of the eighteen wheeler at the truck stop. Ask the over-the-road salesman at the small town restaurant, where he sits next to a local farmer having his mid-morning coffee.

"What's a good pie?"

Guaranteed answer is something like, "Well, Mable here makes a darned good deep dish apple."

Man, you've got it made.

Pass up the creme de broccoli pie or the Chef's masterpiece smothered in whipped cream.

Take the apple.

The Sensitive Guy

Maybe this is the best description of me.

A few years ago I described to an elderly minister friend, how easily emotion came to my eyes, how embarrassingly quickly I reacted to a scene of pathos or the sound of old familiar hymns. Not that I broke down and bawled, mind you, but just a couple of little bitty tears appeared.

His analysis was "I know you well, Bill. It's just that you are super sensitive to peoples' crises and empathize quickly with their emotional pathos. It's a good type of sensitivity and the Lord blesses you with it."

Or is it that I'm just too emotional?

My spouse, Carol, must know, after fifty years together.

Example: when we attended a special program of Cursillo (a Christian religious weekend experience) I quickly became choked up with the emotional mood swing of several hundred people. My singing voice broke when I sang the glorious songs involved, and I sometimes found it hard to talk.

She doesn't. Not at all.

Is it just this Sensitive Guy—a product of a sensitive Irish mother and a very removed English father, or is it my spouse, product of a solid, phlegmatic German mother and Norwegian father?

And if I am indeed that Sensitive Guy, is there anything wrong with that?

The man I follow was a much more Sensitive Guy and a great person.

VICTORIA

The Greatest Compliment

What does it require to be a "good" man?

In the eyes of this boy, my Uncle Pat was one of those good men. In some ways he was just another one of the Hull boys, my father's youngest brother, the son of Sheriff Charlie Hull. But to me he was special.

Pat (a nickname for Clarence) grew up in those halcyon days which turned its back on young men's shenanigans but demanded some semblance of decency and conformity. That was Uncle Pat.

I came along later and knew him first as a young married man—but also the man who broke his neck.

Forty years or more later I did the same thing—broke my neck, that is—so I know some of the agony Pat endured.

His accident was one the family remembered, from the oldest sibling, my dad, to the youngest, my Aunt Geneva.

Pat apparently was always intrigued by speed. Even as a middle-aged man—nay, even before those years—Pat always had a car that would burn up the highways. In this particular instance, I don't know what brand or model he was driving, but I've always pictured it as being a Stutz Bearcat; streamlined, snout-nosed, wire wheels, open top, a real gut buster of a car.

Anyway, I say, as I hitch up my boots to the railing of the pot-bellied stove in the general store, Pat was driving west on the original "old 40," putting the pedal to the metal, splitting the wind. I can see him, pompadoured blonde hair streaming back while he streaked along the country road hellbent for leather.

I know just the exact spot where a farmer pulled out in front of Pat, I think with a team of mules pulling a load. Probably hay. Pat had no choice but to slam into him at 108 miles per hour or whatever was the comparable speed in those days.

And broke his neck!

After the injury was attended, the neck set and braced, his mother, my grandmother, was chastising him properly. "If you hadn't been driving so fast, so recklessly," she went on, "you would never have hit that team and wagon and been hurt."

"Hell, Ma," Pat replied, "If I'd been driving faster I'd have been past that point when that damned fool pulled out in front of me."

Good point.

He was a sportsman. With Mary, he had a place down on the Lake of the Ozarks and always a big super sleek, super powerful outboard motorboat which he liked to drive so fast it slammed into the waves of that big lake with such power that the neophyte thought the boat would disintegrate. I know he once scared the very devil out of my dear meek mother.

He was also a hunter.

I well remember an occasion when this teenager was permitted to join the men on a duck hunt. Pat and others had a hunting shack on the river, atop a bluff which dropped away to the river. Was it the Missouri or the Blackwater? We came in from a rather fruitless (duckless) hunt and picked up our load to carry up that formidable bluff, with saplings every foot apart, up to the shack. As a strong but stupid young teenager, I opted to carry the motor; now if you pick up a 20 hp outboard today it isn't that overpowering, but in those days a 20 hp was made mainly of cast iron and heavy as hell.

Of course I couldn't handle it.

Part way up the hill, as I fought to avoid falling over backwards, there was Pat's strong arm on my back: "Let me have it, Bill; it's too heavy." I always thanked him silently for not saying "too heavy for you." That was kind.

No wonder I darned near worshipped him.

Years later, home from graduate school, I had a chance to go quail shooting with Pat and others. Now, wouldn't you know that Pat had the world's best gun, a Browning automatic, the Cadillac of shotguns at that time. He was an acknowledged good wing shot man at the local gun club.

Versus me. I had an old double-barreled shotgun, Damascus steel barrel of my dad's. I'd never shot at skeet, didn't even know what a skeet "bird" was—but I had qualified as an Expert and as an Instructor in the National Rifle Association's Junior category. And I'd never shot a quail in my life, that fast moving, evasive game that explodes thunderously from cover and rockets away.

To get to the point, several of us were in a row advancing cautiously across an open field when a quail covey flushed before us, a startling event. I pulled up, fired twice quickly, and saw my birds fall to the ground.

Immediately, at my right, Pat spoke up.

"Damn! Bill! How did you ever learn to shoot like that? You beat me to both of them."

Of course that was the greatest compliment, my greatest stroking.

I had outshot Uncle Pat!

Of course he was better than I. He had more experience, more skill, a better gun, and was simply a better hunter.

In summary, Pat had a good life. He probably did everything important in life he wanted to do. He married Mary

Settles, who remembers seeing him with his broken neck in a cast before they even knew each other.

Yes, he had a good life. He and Mary had a lovely daughter, my cousin Evelyn, who married Charlie Brownfield and worked as an elected county official before succumbing early in life to cancer, leaving behind a family.

Pat's end was dramatic too. Always the good guy, always giving of himself, he was cleaning the house gutters at his sister-in-law's home, when the ladder walked away causing him to fall to his death on the driveway.

What else can I say?

Clarence "Pat" Hull was a good man, the perfect Good Ol' Boy.

Trees Split Wide Open

Most of us alive during the nineteen-thirties will remember the drought and the depression; it's almost impossible to forget ninety days of temperatures always at one hundred degrees; and it's just as impossible to forget how hard it was to feed a family if you were a married couple. Fathers took any kind of work they could get, at any amount of money; mothers learned to stretch their meager food supplies by many devious but delicious ways.

In retrospect, I wonder how my mother could afford the dozen or so eggs she would put into her famous angel food cakes. She didn't have chickens in town and our country relatives had to sell the few eggs they could spare in order to buy other food at the stores.

There was another type of weather phenomenon which left its mark on all of us.

That was the ice storm. In the mid-south, like mid-Missouri, we didn't get much snow but we seemed to have a lot of freezing rain.

Now, in those days in the mid-thirties, when rain came in the winter time, it was usually accompanied by freezing weather. Of course the first obvious sign was roads freezing and slickening, so cars went into the ditches, or plowed out of control into trees on the streets.

For example, it was about the winter of 1936–37, but perhaps a year or two later, when we had a storm I will never forget. We had gone to bed hearing the drizzling rain on the roof and knew it was cold; for one thing houses weren't as well insulated then as now. By morning we were being awakened by the cracking of breaking tree limbs and the noise of them falling to the ground.

When daylight came our street was impossible. It was clogged with huge limbs which had broken away from the giant elms and oaks and crashed into the street, over the sidewalks, sometimes onto cars or houses themselves. Dad and I went outside and couldn't believe the great amount of debris in plain sight—just in our immediate neighborhood.

Not only had trees borne so much weight of frozen rain on the limbs that their huge branches snapped off the main trunk, but in some cases the whole tree had split exactly down the middle and half of it was on the ground. It was a horrible thing to see. Madison has always been noted for its fine collection of trees, many a hundred years or more in age. No battlefield could look worse except for the absence of human corpses.

I recall reading Clara Barton's description of the battlefield at the Second Battle of Bull Run near Manassas, at Harper's Ferry, at South Mountain. This lady, who founded the American Red Cross, was called the Angel of the Battlefield for the work she did caring for the soldiers during the Civil War. The battlefield carnage she described was obviously much worse than what we saw all over Madison during that storm and others just like it, because Clara saw so many dead and wounded fighting men, whom she tried to help surgeons save for return to hospitals.*

I hope the reader never has to see beautiful, sturdy old trees encased in ice an inch thick, or small young apple trees crushed to the ground, broken to pieces. We were genuinely overwhelmed at the enormity of the event.

Of course no vehicles moved. Men came out in droves to clean up the mess. Every man had an axe, perhaps even a two-man saw; a few probably had the one man Swede saw as it is called in Minnesota—but everyone worked to clear the streets. It was a massive job and for years its scars were there to be remembered.

---

*Read "NURSE—Heart and Hands," William H. Hull, 1991, ISBN 0-939330-04-0 wherein the author quotes from and refers the reader to "Clara Barton: Professional Angel," by Elizabeth Brown Pryor, University of Pennsylvania Press, © 1987. ISBN 0-8122-8060-1, an excellent reference of the life of this outstanding woman.

On Pets and Veterinarians

Like most boys growing up I had a series of dogs for pets, among which I can remember a couple of fuzzy little bundles of activity which were castoffs from people having larger dogs and looking for someone to take a pup off their hands. But most of those dogs were outside animals and came and went with some regularity.

Until Sammy came along. Now Sammy was a Boston Bulldog—and one says that in capitals because in those days a full blooded, probably pedigreed dog, was unusual because, as I just said, most pups were crossbreeds resulting from free running animals.

Sammy was the pet of my life for many years. He came into our house because my father bought him from someone passing through town, and to pay real out-of-pocket money for a dog in those days, in that area, made the dog quite a gift.

He was different. I'd never had a shorthaired dog and Boston bulldogs have so little hair they seem embarrassingly naked. But they were also very animated and Sammy was typical; he was a ball of fire, an energetic little thing always on the run, with little feet and nails clattering on the floor and little perky ears always at attention.

We probably had Sammy for ten or twelve years, which must have been predominately my younger teen years.

Then, suddenly, he disappeared.

What had happened to my closest friend? He had been let outside and then never came back inside.

The local police thought he had been stolen, probably picked up by some passing tourist. They were right because, after putting out a warning to nearby Columbia, about 25 miles away in those days, the Columbia police located Sammy in a passing tourist's car and returned him to us.

The conclusion was in the minds of authorities that someone had spoken of Sammy's abilities and it had been an intentional dognapping. You see, Sammy had obviously had carnival show dog training because he was anxious to show you that he could perform roll-over-and-play-dead, sit-up-and-beg, and other tricks of a carny dog. So, obviously he had potential and someone was quick to grasp that moment.

Sammy was with us several more years before time took him away and I have good memories of him. In those days in a small town, veterinarians were for farm cattle, not for pets.

The difference was made obvious to my family in many ways over a span of many years. When retired and living on the farm, my father once took his senior mother cat, Fluffy (was it?) into town and actually paid a veterinarian to look her over. It actually embarrassed my father to admit that he would "waste money" (his words) for a cat's visit to a vet.

Then again, at about the same time our daughters had purchased a parakeet while on an auto trip but by the time we arrived home in Minneapolis, the bird was ill with a flu-like disease. We took it to a city veterinarian—who killed it. All four of us well remember that inept veterinarian giving that poor little bird an injection with a needle and syringe that looked huge. To this day we still think he skewered that poor little bird who, immediately after receiving the injection, turned tail and plopped down as dead as it could be.

But don't think this is a diatribe against veterinarians. Years later we had great relations with a fine city vet who cared for our Tobey, a beagle, for many years with great gentleness until the dog's seniority required he be put down.

By the same token I well remember a few months ago when our cat, Brandy, returned to our nearby two-doctor small animal clinic for its annual shots. I particularly remember being in shock at the bill of $84. In my dad's days, the local veterinarian, a large-animal specialist of course, would travel 25 miles or so to the farm and vaccinate dad's white-face cattle for that kind of money.

As I'm frequently quoted as saying, all change is not progress.

The Last of the Line

"About all I do anymore," my dad lamented, "is go to funerals. All of my own generation is gone and I'm the oldest man in the county."

That had to hurt when one realizes he had been born and lived in this same county almost all of his life, excepting for a very few years in Kansas City. He knew everybody and everybody knew him.

But it's Geneva, his sister, and the youngest of the four boys and two girls in their family, excluding for the moment little Madaline who died on her third birthday—it's Geneva I think of mostly these days.

Geneva must frequently contemplate about being the last of the brood. Like my dad, she must view with a heavy heart the funerals of her siblings. There was Pat in 1978, age 71; Seborn in 1980, age 84; Gladys (her only sister) in 1983, age 80; Roy in 1985, age 84; and Aubrey in 1986, age 93.

And here she is, functioning well at age 80 in December 1993, the last of the clan.

She remembers those days of hard work on the farm, when plowing was done with a team of mules, when laundry was a matter of scrubbing your knuckles red on the board, using homemade caustic soap.

She has to remember all of those threshing bees when the grain had to be hand cut with scythes, delivered to the threshing machine by horse drawn wagons, and how filthy the crew was when they came to the house for noontime dinner. And how they ate!

Wringing wet with sweat, chaff down their necks itching like mad, coming to the huge table, sometimes an impromptu one outside, after only a quick rinse at the cistern pump.

As a woman she had to help her mother and older sister cook furiously all morning to feed that tired, ravenous group of family and neighbors. There were big pieces of meat to roast, huge mounds of potatoes to peel and mash, maybe bread or rolls to bake the same day, plus pies and cakes probably made the day before.

There was also a huge garden to tend, to hoe, to debug, sometimes by hand-picking the bugs or worms and dropping them into a jar of kerosene. Then came harvest time when those vegetables needed to be picked, dried, some put in the root cellar, much of it canned in a boiling, steaming kitchen for sustenance next winter.

I saw much of this from the sidelines. There wasn't much for a kid to do, except to keep out of the way and sometimes to fetch a water jug. Mainly we concentrated on swiping a freshly fried chicken drumstick or maybe a conveniently cut piece of apple or gooseberry pie. We knew that when that hungry horde of threshers hit the table, there would be little left over.

Memories!

Geneva must have lots of good ones.

When she attended Aubrey's funeral (my dad) she must have faced memories of their childhood years, of going to school together, the oldest and the youngest, of the great many evenings she and her husband, George, had played cards with my parents, great friends that they were.

She must have remembered that dark and gloomy jail just through the wall from their house in the sheriff's quarters when grandfather wore the big star.

She undoubtedly knows that she represents the end of an era, the beginning of a change.

But don't we all?

Of all those six siblings, most bore girls except the sisters who bore sons named Kramer and Sites. Not a Hull among them, except me. Then here I came along, the only Hull, and I had two daughters. I know this bothered my grandfather because he once said so. Not that he didn't love and appreciate his two lovely new great-granddaughters, he did so badly want someone to carry on his name. Girls! he thought. They can't do that, so my line is dead.

So, Geneva, live many years in peace and harmony with nature. Enjoy your children and grandchildren with whom you are blessed.

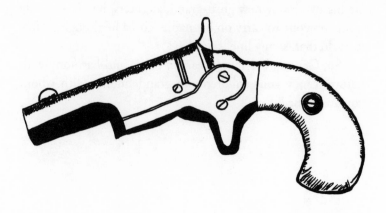

The Derringer

Times were more than tough in the nineteen-thirties when I was a kid in high school. No, "disastrous" may be a more appropriate word.

It was time for me to start thinking of how I was going to get through college. The family couldn't do it financially and, even though I was working for J. C. Penney for the enviable wage of twenty-five cents an hour, it would take a lot of hours, a lot of scholarship money, to make it a go. Then along came Uncle Neil to throw a little light my way.

Uncle Neil was actually my great uncle Cornelius, my grandfather's brother; he had been born in 1860, so now was about seventy years old. He was a nondescript old bachelor who went from Hull family to Hull family to grace them with his presence, invited or not.

When I was about sixteen and laboriously gathering information for a future book by interviewing my grandfather's generation, those old folks were glad to tell me the yarns of the family; they would have talked to anyone who wanted to know what it was like in the good old days, so I just lucked out because of my curiosity.

As it happened, many years later one of my books carried much of that material and was published as "Aunt Zettie's Wonderful Salve." Zettie was one of Neil's sisters and had a secret salve remedy which would cure cuts or warts on man or beast. Her story was in that book, now out of print.

In any event, Uncle Neil liked me and wanted to give me a present. He knew I was interested in hunting and rifles, so one day he very casually gave me a pocket derringer. It was something he had owned for years and it was a marvelous collector's item. I was very grateful and spent much time admiring, but not firing, the weapon. It never went to school with me, as might be the case today, but stayed locked up at home. Mother's strict orders.

Later, along came college days. Although I still had the twenty-five cent job at Penney's, it took a lot of money to commute to school, to buy books, and to have a date on occasion. By that time I was doing anything to earn money, and trying to write and to sell articles. It was indeed tough going.

Of course I looked at the derringer which I knew was worth at least fifty dollars. That was two hundred hours of work at Penney's.

So, God forgive me, I sold the weapon for fifty dollars.

And, of course, the fifty dollars was soon gone. Even though for a quarter you could buy a gallon of gas or a bowl of chili from a restaurant, fifty dollars still didn't last forever. Soon all I had was the memory of that fine old pistol.

As I interviewed all of these oldsters I began to realize the whole family was truly getting old. It was common to see male and female Hulls in their seventies and eighties; they were truly oldsters compared with others of their generation.

So I started collecting birth/death dates and kept doing so until my grandfather's whole generation was gone.

Even then I liked statistics. I still do, when I see age averages of that branch of the Hulls. My great-great grandfather Ebanizer lived to 101. Ebanizer's son, my great grandfather Richard, only made it to 58, vs. his wife, Louisa Jane Swain's 68. But the longevity strain from the two families started a good trend. Their nine children, born between 1857 and 1876 lived to an average of 82.4 years.

That's a long-lived family if there ever was one. William

and Luzetta reached 88, Samantha 86, Charles, (my grandfather) and Cornelius 85, Lydia 82, Arthur 81, John 75, and Lucinda 72. I knew all of these people.

Then came my grandfather's children. He (Charles) had lived to be 85 while his wife, Lillian Ashmead, made it to 76. Their children also set records: Aubrey, my father, reached 93, Seborn 85, Clarence 71 (by accidental death), Leroy 84, Gladys 80, and Geneva still living at 79.

Those five deceased siblings averaged 82.6 years each.

When we put it all together: Ebanizer 101, Richard 58, Richard's 9 children 742 years, Charles' 3 children—249 years, (not counting Leroy, Gladys, or Geneva)—average 82 years each.

But what about the next, my generation, the children of my father's generation? It's too early to tell. Nine reached adulthood, with my brother Charles dying at age 10 and ignored in these statistics. Two are now deceased, Elaine at 63, Evelyn at 59, an average of 56. The remaining seven: Richard Kramer 45, Kay Kramer Coen 48, Wanda Davis 52, George Kramer Jr. 57, Tom Sites 58, June Hull Kempf 60, and William 75. These seven living people average 56.3 years each.

But the wives of my great grandfather (Louisa, 68 years) and of my grandfather (Lillian, 76 years) didn't add to the longevity of their children's generations.

But even at that, I personally must have some good genes coming from the Hull family.

But, alas, there's also my mother's family genes, which aren't so good.

On my mother's side, I can go back only to my great grandfather, who is just a name, Adam Cornelius, with no life span information, so I must start with his daughter, my great grandmother. Margaret Melissa Cornelius, who lived to be 62, married Patrick Henry Donohoe, who made it to 75, but of their 7 children we only have lifespans for five whose spans totaled 285 years. Lucinda Catherine (my maternal grand-mother) 77, Peter 52, Cornelius 50, William 20, and Charlie and John, stats unknown. However, those five averaged 57 years.

Then came my mother's generation, children of Lucinda Catherine and William Franklin Moore. Eleven of them lived 582 years, or an average of 52.9 years. They were Joseph 76, Mary (my mother) 72, Willa 65, Monroe 60, Walter (a twin) 57, Charlie (the other twin) 51, Fannie 50, Bob 46, Leslie 43, Gertrude 42 and Dolly 20. There's no longevity to be proud of in that family.

Adding them all together, like we did for the Hulls, we get: great grandmother 62, her five children 285, Lucinda Catherine's eleven children, 582. That's a total of 17 Moore family people living 929 years, or an average of 54.6 years each.

But what's the bottom line?

Simply that the Hull family has outlived the Moore family by 50%. That's an average of 82 years for the Hulls and 54.6 for the Moores.

But how easy it is to jump to erroneous conclusions!

For example, my father should never have lived to be 93 years old. Why? Because of what he ate.

Eggs from free running farm chickens for most of his breakfasts, and fried at that. Bacon or ham, country cured and delicious, but cured with salt. All the fat he wanted and he was very fond of it from a pork roast. All the black coffee he could drink. Pure country cream for years on his breakfast cereal; whole milk later when he moved to town. And sweets! Lord, how he liked my mother's pies and cakes, and a special German leppe cookie, made of sorghum molasses at Christmas time and kept in a tin for a month or so.

All of that was offset by hard physical work all of his life, plus very limited use of alcohol and tobacco.

Now, along comes my generation. We don't work nearly

as hard physically but we have stress unlike these previous generations knew; and we have the advantage of knowing how harmful to us can be the foods we have learned to eat all of our lives. I can't believe we will ever live to the ripe old ages of those previous generations, in spite of what the insurance tables and medical doctors tell us.

When I look back at my boyhood, it seems that all I did was go to funerals.

I was born in 1918 during the big flu outbreak, my birth following by two days the death of a baby cousin; this event must have been most traumatic for my pregnant mother. By the time I was ten my great uncle Peter Donohoe had died (1923), my beloved grandmother, Catherine Donohoe Moore (1938), and my uncle Monroe Moore (1939), all on my mother's side of the family. Only four in that decade, but foreboding what would occur in the next ten-year span.

In the 1940s, which were my twenties, my marriage and two children years, I lost my dear uncle Charlie Moore (1941), great uncle Jim Donohoe (1942), great uncle Cornelius Hull (1945), great uncle by marriage Lou Haller (1946), my cousin Joseph Davis and my dear uncle Bob Moore (both in 1947), my lovely grandmother Lillian Hull and great aunt Lydia Haller (both in 1948) and my aunt by marriage, Minnie Coffman Moore (1949). This was a group of ten people in ten years.

The 1950s were my thirties, my initial years in the publishing business and the switch to deaths among my father's side of the family. We lost great aunt Zettie Steger and great aunt Manth Cattrell (both in 1950), my stalwart grandfather, Charles Hull (1953) and two of his brothers, great uncle Arth Hull (1957) and great uncle Will Hull (1958).

Again, in the 60s, we saw a dearth of deaths on my mother's side—my aunt Willa Jeffress (1961), cousin John Haller Jr., (1961), uncle by marriage Walter Davis (1963), cousin Silas Moore (1964), cousin Joseph Jeffress (1965), my ad-

mired uncle Joseph Roscoe Moore (1965), my own dear
mother, Mary Moore Hull (1966), uncle by marriage Homer
Jeffress (1966), second cousin Jack Donohoe (1966), and
cousin Dorothy Jeffress (1967).

The 70s were my major business years, very much on the
go, raising two daughters and seeing the Hulls beginning to
disappear. There was my beloved aunt Flora Hull (1972), second cousin Bertha Haller Hagelin (1974), my greatly admired uncle Pat Hull and my great aunt by marriage Bess
Hull (both in 1978), second cousin Sylvester Haller (1979),
dear aunt by marriage Sara Howard Moore (1978) and aunt
by marriage Helene Moore (1979).

Ah, but the 80s, during which my father's siblings died
aplenty and I faced retirement as I became the older generation. The world lost my beloved uncle Seborn Hull (1980),
lovely aunt Gladys Sites (1983), aunt by marriage Fannie
Davis Moore (1984), admired uncle Roy Hull (1985), my
fine father Aubrey Hull (1986), uncle by marriage John Sites
(1986), dear cousin Elaine Hull Duren (1987), and great
uncle Will Donohoe (1988). That decade made a big dent in
my father's generation.

The 90s saw everything coming to a close as far as those
generations were concerned. Already we've lost aunt by marriage, Florence Walje Moore (1990), cousin Homer Jeffress
Jr. (1991), and aunt by marriage Ruth Stewart Hull (1992).

Of course these are the natural chain of events. As generations die, new generations are born and while families may
disperse to the ends of the earth, their lineage does not actually disappear.

Now can the reader see what I meant words ago when I
said it seemed that all I did as a boy was to go to funerals?
And the pattern never stopped.

The Prophylactic

Modern young people may prefer I call it a condom, but that's a relatively new word. Napoleon, George Washington and generations in this country called them rubbers, but it was traditionally preferred to point to a "package of those" so the druggist would know what was wanted.

You see, the condom was unknown by that name, a word that didn't exist until a St. Louis, Missouri, latex rubber glove manufacturer, George C. Condom, had an idea how we could use the imperfect rubber gloves that sometimes appeared in his production line. It wasn't long before he had packaged these items and had them for sale in men's rest rooms in dispensing machines all up and down U.S. Highway 40, now I-70.

This had apparently occurred about 1940 when "the U.S. Public Health Service argued the urgent need for schools to get involved (in sex education)."*

Now old George was no fool. He put his name on every single dispensing machine and on each package, labeled "Condom's." He wasn't so foolish as to use the word as an adjective; he came right out and labeled them "condoms" (notice, no possessive mark) with the next line reading "For Protection Against Disease."

The problem was that George had caught syphilis in his younger days, before condoms were marketed; he died at 104 years in pain but he was a very wealthy man.**

* TIME, May 24, 1993, p. 62.

**The article from which this story was taken was in a book or magazine located in the Southdale Hennepin Area Library of Edina (MN) and originally interpreted by me that the whole article came from the aforementioned issue of TIME, which was not true. In discussions with TIME personnel between January 20 and March 7, 1994, by mail and by telephone, I sought permission to quote the original source as being TIME, but was assured it was not TIME/LIFE property and I did not need their permission to quote all or part of it. Authority: Ms. Edith Rosa, TIME/LIFE, New York, by telephone, March 7, 1994. I have been unable to retrace my steps to find the original source, in which the error was apparently made. For one thing, that particular library has been closed for two months during this period.

Being a reliable researcher, in an attempt to verify or refute this story, I have been in contact with the Missouri Historical Society in St. Louis, Missouri, where a kind lady, Emily Miller, went the extra mile trying to help. She checked archives, manuscript catalogs, files of trade catalogs, city directories, and other well-indexed sources, finding no reference to George C. Condom. Also, the State Historical Society of Missouri, at Columbia, Missouri, Marie Concannon, reference specialist, was very helpful, checking many sources, but also being unable to either confirm nor deny the authenticity of this story.

Hence I, William Hull, decided to leave the story in the book, with this warning that it may be entirely untrue, but with the wish I could confirm the original source.

Aunt Zettie's Wonderful Salve

Aunt Zet was my father's aunt, Luzetta Jane Hull Steger, daughter of Richard Romulus Hull, born January 10, 1862. She was old.

I remember her well. When I was ten, she was an ancient sixty-six, living in Pilot Grove next door to my Grandmother Moore. Her husband, Uncle Jim Steger, was a woodworking genius and I can visualize his tool shed behind the house. It was filled with hand and foot powered tools. There was a foot powered lathe and all the tools early craftsmen had to use. Primitive as they seem today, they were a source of intrigue for a ten-year-old boy. Of course there was no electricity.

Aunt Zet was a warm and comforting person, always kind to us children and overflowing with love. And cookies.

To my mother she was also a true friend. I sensed more than a casual liking between the two of them, a mutual respect, perhaps born of something that had occurred many years previously. Of course Zet had lived next to the Moores when my mother was a girl before mother and dad had eloped from that little village by taking a train to Sedalia, getting married, returning the same day and telling no one of their marriage for several days.

Aunt Zet was noted, among other things, for possessing a salve that could heal cuts, sores, abrasions, faster than anything available in the rather primitive drug stores existing then. Her homemade salve was something to treasure and to hoard for those hard-to-heal sores that seemed so numerous.

She made this remedy, bottled it in pharmacy jars and gave it away to friends. Never would she sell any of it. It was just a gift.

Everybody wanted Aunt Zet's salve recipe but, for some reason, she didn't pass it out indiscriminately. But, before she died in 1950, at the age of 88, she passed it on to my mother, as the caretaker of her valuable cure-all. My mother valued the recipe as a personal treasure. Forty-two years after Aunt Zet's death, I found the recipe in my mother's prized possessions, written on the flap of an envelope, which she had apparently used to take down the recipe many years previously.

Here it is in its complete form:

Take equal parts of beeswax, rosin,* lard and mutton tallow. Melt slowly and mix well. Pour into containers and let cool.

Just try, dear reader, to obtain some of these ingredients today. It was indeed a treasure . . . this recipe nearly a hundred years old.

That should take care of one's sores, boils and wounds on horses and humans for quite a spell.

---

*Rosin is a resin from pine trees used in making varnish, soldering flux and on violin bows. (Webster's Ninth Collegiate Dictionary.)

Spilling His Guts

For the effete, the sensitive, the ladies and gentlemen, I apologize profusely for this distasteful title. I've used it intentionally after reminiscing about the way hogs used to be transformed into bacon and hams on the farm.

It may be that some farmers, particularly pig farmers, may still today in certain geo-regions actually butcher some of their own animals, but it must be a rare procedure in most areas. It's not a peculiarly pleasurable procedure but is effective and cost saving, so who can criticize the skilled person who prefers to do it at home.

Because I had seen hogs butchered on the farm as a kid, it wasn't terribly repulsive for me to dress out my own game when I started deer hunting, after moving to Minnesota in 1946.

I'm not a member of the National Rifle Association, having given up that group years ago, but I've enjoyed hunting game for the table for many years. But, I must admit, there's nothing quite as memorable as seeing an animal dressed out for food. Once seen, always remembered.

At this point I must digress to tell of my last successful deer hunt, which was via shotgun slug in a large county park, the result of a successful permit drawing by me. I had killed my deer when it appeared at the edge of a copse of woods while I sat on the ground leaning against a tree at the top of a hill forty yards away. I descended to the downed animal and

was dressing it out when a voice directly behind me said, "Hello, may I watch?" That surprised me because each hunter was supposed to stay in his own assigned territory and not wander around. Of course I let him watch, because, as he said, he had never dressed out a deer nor even seen it done.

We talked as I worked. He learned that I was recovering from a heart attack, that my van was up over the hill from which I had shot and it was obvious I had to drag that big doe up that wooded, rocky slope and get it into my van. So he knew the situation.

When nearly finished, he suddenly remarked, "Well, thanks. I've got to go." And he did! I was so astounded I didn't think quickly enough to shout, "Wait up! Help me get this doe up the hill and into the van." I should have spoken up.

I managed to move it myself, pulling that large deer up that hill, getting hung up in small brush, finally reaching the opened rear doors of the van. Let me assure you the hardest thing to handle, the most awkward item in the world is the warm relaxed carcass of a large animal. It's like moving a huge chunk of Jello.* I made it eventually but my opinion of young hunters wasn't too rosy for a couple of days.

I had first witnessed a butchering at Uncle Seb's when I was somewhere between eight and eleven. I think it was a shoat (a young hog probably less than a year old) and had been knocked on the head, hung up by the rear legs against the outside wall of the barn and its throat slashed to bleed quickly, which is a must for any meat.

The blood rushed onto the ground, to be wasted because this family didn't make blood sausage as did some families. Then the most revolting part occurred. Uncle Neil took the huge butcher knife and split the carcass from groin to throat so all the whitish intestines were immediately disgorged onto the ground. Quickly I lost my breakfast and then decided I was not needed around there anymore.

The crew used those big old steel butcher knives, some with oak handles, for cutting the pork into pieces like the ribs, tenderloins, ham, shoulders, bacon or even sow belly. Later, when we were married we purchased a Sheffield steel butcher knife which lasted us for household use for at least twenty-five years until it simply disappeared.

The hair had to be singed to remove it from the hide. In olden days that was accomplished by bringing a large amount of water to a boil in an open container, like an iron pot over an outdoor fire. Of course that took hours of heating over that fire and also required a block and tackle, probably over a large tripod of smaller wooden trees to lift and move the carcass so it could be dipped. After dipping in the scalding water, the entire skin had to be scraped to remove the unwanted hair which no one wanted on their ham or bacon. Sometimes every member of a family was conscripted to help scrape.

Recently I read of a newly recommended method of butchering at home—the easy way. The entire process was performed on the ground, never lifting the carcass. The animal was slaughtered with a 22 caliber rifle shot between the eyes, or a blow to the head with an axe; then it was bled and eviscerated on the ground, where it fell. If the area became too messy, the butcher was instructed to roll the hog over onto boards and proceed. To remove the hair/bristles it was suggested heating the skin to the point of blistering with a butane torch, after which the skin was scraped with something like an old garden hoe, an old one being less prone to cut the hide than a sharp new one would be. The carcass was then to be washed and the backbone split with an axe.

Whew. Sounds dirty to me.

After butchering, some of that meat was consumed within a day or two, much was cut up and made into sausage, either bulk or in casings. To this day my Aunt Geneva Hull Kramer still cans cooked meat, such as pork. I've eaten this "put up" meat and found it excellent; it was a good way to save meat for future use.

But it was the smoke house which drew the hams and the bacon sides, maybe even the shoulders, which were sort of an inferior ham; they were cured with a combination of salt, heavily rubbed into the meat, and lengthy smoking from special woods. The smoke house was just what the name implied, an entirely separate building on the farm, wherein the hams and bacon were hung from the rafters to provide plenty of exposure to the smoke filling the room. That smoke also discouraged flies, particularly in the fall when fly populations were low. Even then, there were times when a female fly could get to the meat, lay her eggs and the resulting maggots would hatch out to "blow" the meat. Usually the meat had to be destroyed, but during the depression of the thirties it was rumored that certain hungry people cut away the maggots and cooked the remainder of the meat. Ugh!

Today's alternatives for a smoke house include smoking in an old refrigerator. Many fishermen smoke their fish and some people smoke other meats in a reworked refrigerator placed outdoors. The procedure necessitates providing a bottom inlet for air and an outlet at the top. Inside, at the bottom a small burner is placed with a covering grate, upon which is slowly heated select sawdust to provide smoke. A caution says the sawdust must be kept damp to assure smoke rather than flames. The whole procedure must take place outside.

But, oh, how wonderful that meat can be. There are very few scents which can throw most of us and our appetites into high gear. Those are the smell of bacon/ham frying, the smell of coffee being made, or the smell of bread baking in the oven.

---

*Registered brand of Kraft General Foods, Inc., White Plains, NY 10625.

VICTORIA

An Angry Father

In 1858 Lincoln had said in a debate, probably with Stephen A. Douglas, "I believe this government cannot endure permanently half slave and half free," which was really a call to end slavery. Then, after he won the presidency and took office, very quickly Southern states began to leave the union.

Then when he issued the proclamation of emancipation for negroes in September 1862, followed in December 1865 by the 13th Amendment to the Constitution, slavery was ended in the United States.

This soon meant division of families, of homes, with sons actually going to battle with opposing forces, fathers and sons sometimes being in close combat. In some states, like the border state of Missouri, which truly was split down the middle, that meant some very unhappy family members.

In recent years my father owned a piece of land, a small piece of a very large tract owned at one time by a very wealthy man. When that man learned of his serious illness in 1887, he decided to write his personal will and to include it in the legal land papers, title or whatever. It is a remarkable notice because it shows how deeply hurt and angered the father had been.

As usual, in the first place, he directed the payment of his existing debts, after which his wife was to receive "one third of my real and personal estate absolutely." Then to his son

Bram, $500—which today doesn't sound like much for a wealthy man to leave a son. Then comes the first sign of anger when he said, "To my daughter, Mary, I give the sum of $400, but her husband has been a rebel against this government; I desire that this small amount shall be invested and so managed that my said daughter shall alone receive the benefit of it during their joint lives, and in no event to be subject to the payment of his debts." So there! Son-in-law.

Then, fifthly, "I give to my daughter-in-law, Mary Frances, the wife of my son William, the sum of $200, this sum to be subject to her control and management."

Now, once again, he wants to make a major point:

"Sixthly, as all the children of my first wife inherited from their grandfather a right pretty estate, and which like all other fools they have done all in their power to destroy by the acts of treason and disloyalty to their Government (The best ever established among men) and for the further reason that my three oldest sons, William, Bingham and John, have been wilfully disobedient and unmindful of my best counsel and advice and have sought and followed the advice and counsel of evil, wicked and traitourously affected persons, and they thereby destroyed more than half of my estate, I do therefore and for these reasons, give to said sons William and John each the sum of $1.00 and to Bingham the sum of 10 cents, which is all I intend them to have of my estate."

(Guess who is the Union man in this family?)

"Seventhly, I give to my daughter Dotia Ann and my son Abner each one third of the remainder of my estate with my blessings and prayers, that they may increase it honestly and use it wisely and that they may never in their bosoms give shelter to a single thought at (of) war with the union of the States."

"Eighthly, I have one request to make to those who may have the disposition of my body, after death. I have long observed with pain and regret the pride and pomp displayed on funeral occasions, sometimes almost to impoverishment of the living. I want none of it, but direct that my body be interred in the cheapest, plainest and quietest grave; let a plain block of native marble, limestone, mark the spot with my name cut on it and the words "He loved his whole country" and lastly I have hereby constituted my wife executrix of my last will and testament."

It was signed, sealed, witnessed and filed in the county records of March 23, 1887.

Here was a man who had very strong and definite feelings about the differences causing that war.

You Clean up Real Good

The daffodils were all gone but the azaleas, the dogwood, and particularly the wisteria were at their peak when we were in Jackson, Mississippi, in March to see them, along with other members of The Men's Garden Clubs of America.

We had been climbing the paths of a beautiful old estate that warm spring afternoon. Yes, it was warm enough to bring a little sweat to the brow and the armpits as we soaked in nature's great display. Also, the wind had blown us around a little, so it was a somewhat mussed up crowd that was bused back to the hotel. Then we prepared for a reception line, an open bar, and 310 people standing in line to greet the new national officers.

From jeans and short-sleeved shirt I had showered and changed to a dark suit, white shirt and tie for the evening.

As we stood in line, an unknown lady came up behind me and touched me on the shoulder and said, "You clean up real good."

Elsewhere in this book I have written "The Greatest Compliment." Maybe "You clean up real good" was actually the greatest compliment, but maybe it was the greatest put down and I was too egoistic to realize it.

I know that lady realized she was using a grammatically faulty expression, perhaps repeating a homespun or even a backwoods expression, but it was more than cute and flattered me. She knew the word should have been the adverb "well" not "good." She was no sportsman or sports announcer saying "He pitched real good" or one who spoke of "athaleets." This lady was funning me, and I liked it. The next time I see a friend nicely dressed up I'm going to tell him/her "You clean up real good."

Index

YOU'LL LIKE WILLIAM HULL'S
OTHER BOOKS TOO

All books are "trade" size which means they are larger than a paperback, but still not hardbound. Size 8½ × 5¼ inches.

All Hell Broke Loose
Contains experiences of young people during the Armistice Day 1940 blizzard in Minnesota, which killed 59 people. 167 Minnesotans tell how they coped with the storm that killed so many neighbors. Over 500 people were interviewed and selected experiences were included. Best seller in Minnesota for several years. 236 pages.

The Dirty Thirties
Young people tell how they stayed alive during the depression and drought years of the 1930s. The author shares with you the experiences of 147 people from twenty-one states who lived through these terrible years. People who tell 151 different stories. Some humor and photographs. 262 pages.

Nurse: Hearts & Hands
Nurses tell us of their victories and their losses in dealing with patients. They reveal great moments of love and affection for their patients and the reciprocal from their patients. This book will help you evaluate the work done by nurses but will also entertain you as you read of their lives and challenges. 235 pages.

The Good Ol' Boys
The story of Billy Boy, a lad growing up in a small midwestern town in the twenties and thirties, of his experiences with others and of his development into manhood. Herein are shown the influences which shaped his life and personality. Written in a conversational, easy-to-read style.

YOU MAY OBTAIN HULL'S BOOKS FROM ANY BOOKSTORE—or by ordering direct from the author, using this order form:

We suggest that you photocopy or cut out this form, rather than tearing it out and destroying your book.

Send the form and payment to William H. Hull, 6833 Creston Road, Edina, MN 55435. Books autographed to you or for gift purposes if requested.

- -

ORDER FORM

PLEASE SEND ME THE FOLLOWING:

_____ Copies of *All Hell Broke Loose* at $8.95 each: $_____

_____ Copies of *The Dirty Thirties* at $9.95 each: $_____

_____ Copies of *Nurse: Hearts & Hands* at $9.95 each: $_____

_____ Copies of *The Good Ol' Boys* at $11.95 each: $_____

Sub total: $_____

Minnesota residents add 6.5% for state sales tax: $_____

Pluse $2.00 shipping/handling FOR EACH BOOK: $_____

Total enclosed: $_____

Name: _____

Complete Address _____

_____

Prices subject to change